Plant the
Seed

SHARING THE GOSPELS
WITH CHILDREN

Plant the
Seed

SHARING THE GOSPELS
WITH CHILDREN

PATRICIA MATHSON

Liguori

ONE LIGUORI DRIVE
LIGUORI MO 63057-9999

Imprimi Potest: Harry Grile, CSsR, Provincial
Denver Province, The Redemptorists

Published by Liguori Publications
Liguori, Missouri 63057

To order, call 800-325-9521
www.liguori.org

Library of Congress Cataloging-in-Publication Data

Mathson, Patricia L.
 Plant the seed : sharing the Gospels with children / Patricia Mathson.
  p. cm.
 ISBN 978-0-7648-2009-0
 1. Bible. N.T. Gospels--Study and teaching--Catholic Church. 2. Christian education of
children. I. Title.
 BS2556.M35 2011
 226.0071--dc22

                       2010052554

Liguori Publications, a nonprofit corporation, is an apostolate of the Redemptorists. To
learn more about the Redemptorists, visit Redemptorists.com.

Printed in the United States of America
14 13 12 11   5 4 3 2 1
First Edition

Contents

Introduction

Plant the Seed: Sharing the Gospels With Children is filled with engaging, creative ways to encourage children to live the Word of God by sharing the Gospels in ways that speak to their hearts. The Gospels' stories of Jesus show us how God wants us to live; if we help the Gospels come alive for children, they can live as Jesus' disciples.

The twenty-eight stories in this book are drawn from all four Gospels and are presented with a fresh, child-friendly perspective. To help you integrate this material into your curriculum or family faith-sharing time, each lesson suggests themes and seasons in which the lesson could be used.

Each lesson approaches a Gospel story in a comprehensive way:

- The lessons are designed to be used easily when working with children—you can read right from the page!

- Each story is introduced with questions and material that set the scene.

- A kid-friendly meditation personalizes each story. As you read the story aloud, children close their eyes and imagine themselves in the Gospel, inviting Jesus to speak to their hearts.

- Questions reinforce the main idea of each story and invite discussion about its major themes. After you answer the children's questions, reflect on the story and wrap up the discussion.

- A variety of learning activities help the children see how the Gospel relates to their lives. These activities are especially appropriate for children in grades kindergarten through third but can be used with other ages and in intergenerational groups. Service projects, role playing, arts and crafts, new ways of praying, and other activities appeal to children and are easy to implement. Many of the activities work no matter how small or how large the group.

- Each section concludes with a prayer that can be recited as a group or that can be divided into leader and assembly parts. The prayers may be photocopied from the page and shared with the class (see page 4 for photocopying guidelines).

Designed to meet the needs of all who share the Good News of Jesus Christ with children and families, *Plant the Seed* is a great resource for catechists and parents alike. I hope you find that it helps you plant the seed of the Word of God in the hearts and minds of your children.

CHAPTER 1

Sharing the Gospel of Matthew

Share Background With Students

In the Gospel of Matthew, we see that Jesus came to fulfill God's promise to his people. Jesus—the Messiah—proclaims the Good News that the kingdom of God is at hand.

Through the stories in this Gospel, Jesus teaches us how to be his disciples. He shows us how to live as people of the kingdom and work for peace and justice for all. Jesus' life is an example of how we are capable of living: We see Jesus as a person of prayer, and he shows us the importance of prayer in our lives.

Most important, Jesus shows us the Father's love for each of us and stresses that we are to love God with all our hearts. Loving God involves loving others as well, and Jesus expands our idea of what loving others is all about. It means loving others as we love ourselves, even those who don't love us back. Jesus shows us that he came for all people and all nations and all cultures. He challenges us to see him in people in need and to reach out to those who need a helping hand.

As a Church community, we are called to proclaim the Good News of Jesus Christ as we hear it in the Gospel of Matthew. We are to live as Jesus taught us through his words and his actions; in this way, as examples of God's love and messengers of God's hope, we show Jesus to others.

Follow the Star

MATTHEW 2:1–2, 9–11

CHRISTMAS • EPIPHANY • PEACE • FOLLOWING JESUS

When Jesus was born in Bethlehem of Judea, in the days of King Herod, behold, magi from the east arrived in Jerusalem, saying, "Where is the newborn king of the Jews? We saw his star at its rising and have come to do him homage."

After their audience with the king they set out. And behold, the star that they had seen at its rising preceded them, until it came and stopped over the place where the child was. They were overjoyed at seeing the star, and on entering the house they saw the child with Mary his mother. They prostrated themselves and did him homage. Then they opened their treasures and offered him gifts of gold, frankincense, and myrrh.

Introduce the Gospel Story

Do you ever look at the stars at night? Are some stars brighter than others?

Today we hear about the wise men who came to worship Jesus. These wise men studied the stars. They came from far away and followed the brightest star to Jesus. We, too, are to follow the star of Jesus where it leads us.

Share a Meditation

Imagine you're with the wise men. Close your eyes and picture the scene.

You live far away in a strange land. People in your town called the wise men study the stars. One dark night, you're outside with the wise men looking at the stars. Suddenly, one of them notices a bright new star. You look where he is pointing and see that star shining in the night sky. The wise men say the star is a sign that something wonderful has happened!

The wise men talk and decide to follow the star, which will surely lead them to the Messiah—the newborn king. It will be a long journey, but you want to go with them!

The wise men pack up everything they need for the journey and invite you to help them bring along special gifts for the Messiah.

The trip begins, and you travel for miles and miles. Each night your group makes camp, and each morning you set out again. The light of the bright star guides the way. When you look at the star, you wonder what you'll find at the end of the journey.

Finally, the wise men stop beneath the star and unpack the gifts they brought for Jesus. You follow them inside the house. There you find Jesus and his mother, Mary. The wise men are so excited to see Jesus that they fall to their knees in front of him. You do, too, as you gaze in wonder at this special child. Together you and the wise men praise God for the baby Jesus.

Then the wise men offer Jesus their gifts. You know in your heart that the long journey was worth it.

Think about what gift you could give Jesus from your heart. Speak silently now to Jesus and tell him. What does Jesus say to you?

When you're ready, open your eyes. Do any of you want to tell what gift you gave Jesus?

Ask Questions

- Who were the wise men? What did they study?
- What sign did they see in the sky?
- Why did they decide to take a long journey?
- What did the wise men do when they saw Jesus?
- Should we give gifts to Jesus too? What gifts does Jesus want from us?
- Based on this story, whom do we think Jesus came to see? Does he only want to meet people in his family and town, or does he want to meet all people—even those who live far away?

Reflect and Wrap Up the Discussion

The wise men traveled from a distant country to meet Jesus. This story helps us remember that Jesus came for people of all nations and cultures. The wise men's story is our story too. We are on a journey of faith. We must open our hearts to the light of Christ. We must follow the star of Jesus Christ where it leads us.

Craft Activity

MAKE MOSAIC STARS

Materials
- Sheets of yellow craft foam
- Sheets of self-stick craft foam in other colors
- Scissors

Adult Preparation
1. Cut large stars from yellow craft foam.
2. Cut self-stick foam into small squares that fit inside the stars.

Directions for Children

We can decorate these yellow stars with colorful squares. Peel off the backing and stick the colorful squares on your star.

These mosaic stars will remind us that we are to be like the wise men who followed a bright star to Jesus. We must follow the star of Jesus in our lives.

Take your star home and share the story of the wise men with your family.

Pray Together

Lord Jesus Christ,
as we remember the journey of the wise men,
help us search for your star in our lives.
May we go where you lead us
as the light of our lives and the light of our world.
Help us remember you came
for all people and all nations.
May we always live in peace with one another
at all times and in all places. Amen.

From *Plant the Seed: Sharing the Gospel With Children* (Liguori Publications, © 2011 Patricia Mathson). Permission to reproduce granted to original purchaser for noncommercial use only.

Live in Peace

MATTHEW 5:21–22

PEACE • LOVING OUR NEIGHBOR • ANGER
FORGIVENESS • RECONCILIATION

You have heard that it was said to your ancestors, "You shall not kill; and whoever kills will be liable to judgment." But I say to you, whoever is angry with his brother will be liable to judgment.

. . . .

Introduce the Gospel Story

Did you ever feel angry with someone? Does God want us to be angry or to hold grudges?

Today's story is about living in peace with others. Because God makes us one community of friendship, we can't say we love God if we don't live in peace with others.

Jesus tells us to be forgiving and merciful just like God, and he also teaches us to ask forgiveness from people we have hurt.

Share a Meditation

Close your eyes. Imagine you're with Jesus on a hillside.

Jesus is teaching the people. You listen carefully to what he has to say because his words always touch your heart. He reminds you about the commandment that we should not kill. Then Jesus tells you this also means we shouldn't be angry with one another or hold grudges.

Wow! You think that sounds hard to do. But you understand that Jesus is teaching you how to do the right thing. You know that anger and grudges hurt us and others. Jesus is calling us to change our hearts and to love doing what is right.

Keep thinking about what Jesus is saying. He also means that we can't make excuses for what we've done wrong. We have to admit when we sin and ask forgiveness. We also have to forgive others even if they don't ask us for it. Jesus is asking us to let go of hurts and let him change our hearts to love what is good.

Jesus is walking toward you. You think of the people you've hurt. Jesus comes and sits by you. What do you say? What does Jesus say to you?

Our meditation has ended, and you can open your eyes. Do any of you want to share what you talked to Jesus about?

Ask Questions

- ● *In this story, what does Jesus teach about anger?*
- ● *What are ways to calm down when we're angry?*
- ● *Is it easy to let go of grudges? Why or why not?*
- ● *Why is it important to forgive others?*
- ● *Should we forgive people who don't ask our forgiveness?*

Reflect and Wrap Up the Discussion

Jesus calls us to be people of forgiveness so we can live in peace with others. We must ask forgiveness of other people we've hurt with our words or actions. This is what it means to live as the people of God.

We must also forgive people who have hurt us even if they don't ask us to. We can't hold grudges because they only hurt us and keep us from becoming who God created us to be. Peace in our world begins with us!

Craft Activity

CREATE A PEACE DOVE

Materials
- Poster board
- Markers
- Writing paper and pencils

Adult Preparation
1. On the poster board, outline a large dove.
2. Above the dove, write the words "Live in Peace."

Directions for Children

God created us to live in peace with one another. This Gospel is a challenge, but we're to live what Jesus teaches us. Think of ways to live in peace with other people. Here are some ideas:

- **Respect**...the rights of other people
- **Listen**...to what others have to say
- **Forgive**...people who have hurt us
- **Help**...people in difficult circumstances
- **Let go**...of grudges
- **Pray**...for peace in our world

1. Write some "peace words" on the paper in front of you.
2. Then come forward and write one of your peace words with a colorful marker inside the dove. It's OK if some of you have the same word.

Each time we see the peace dove we worked on together, we'll be reminded to live in peace with others!

Pray Together

Spirit of peace,
help us live in peace in our families,
our neighborhoods, our communities, and our world.
Enable us to turn away from hatred and violence
toward the light of your love.
Teach us to forgive those who make us angry,
to ask forgiveness of those we've hurt,
and to make up for the harm we've caused others.
Guide our hearts and our lives into your peace.
We know that with you all things are possible. Amen.

From *Plant the Seed: Sharing the Gospel With Children* (Liguori Publications, © 2011 Patricia Mathson). Permission to reproduce granted to original purchaser for noncommercial use only.

Trust in Jesus
MATTHEW 8:23–27

FEAR • TRUSTING GOD • GOD'S LOVE

He got into a boat and his disciples followed him. Suddenly a violent storm came up on the sea, so that the boat was being swamped by waves; but he was asleep. They came and woke him, saying, "Lord, save us! We are perishing!" He said to them, "Why are you terrified, O you of little faith?" Then he got up, rebuked the winds and the sea, and there was great calm. The men were amazed and said, "What sort of man is this, whom even the winds and the sea obey?"

. . . .

Introduce the Gospel Story

Have you ever been afraid? What happened? Who helped you?

In this Gospel story the disciples were afraid, but they learned to trust Jesus. The story takes place in a boat on the Sea of Galilee. It has an important message: We can trust God even when times are difficult.

Share a Meditation

Bow your head or close your eyes. Get ready to put yourself in this story.

You're with Jesus and his disciples by the Sea of Galilee on a cloudy day. Jesus and his disciples get into a boat. You find a seat on one of the hard, wooden benches. The disciples row the boat way out into the water.

It's quiet out here and peaceful. Many people have fallen asleep—even Jesus! But suddenly the wind gets stronger and the waves become higher, tossing the boat around. It's a storm! You're afraid, and so are the disciples.

They go over to Jesus and wake him. "Lord, save us," they plead. Jesus says, "Why are you afraid? Do you not have faith in me?" Then Jesus gets up and calms the sea and the waves. The storm goes away, and the sun comes out again. The disciples are amazed, and so are you.

You know in your heart that Jesus is God, as he says. He can heal people, and he can calm the storm. You know you can trust Jesus. He'll be with you in the storms and difficult times. He'll be there when you're afraid and when everything seems to be going wrong.

Take a moment now to talk to Jesus in your heart and tell him you have faith in him. Hear what he says to you.

Now open your eyes. Do any of you want to share what Jesus said to you?

Ask Questions
- Why did Jesus and the disciples go out on the water?
- Why were the disciples afraid?
- What did Jesus do to help them?
- What does this story teach us about trusting in God?
- Why is it good to pray when we're afraid?

Reflect and Wrap Up the Discussion
Like the disciples, we must learn to trust Jesus and have faith in God in all times and places. This story helps us remember Jesus is with us always. He's here in the good times *and* the bad times.

We can pray to Jesus when we're afraid or having a bad day. Jesus will hear our prayers like he heard the disciples during the storm. Jesus loves each of us, and he is always with us.

Role-Play Activity
ACT THE GOSPEL STORY
Volunteers Needed
- Jesus (pretends to be asleep, then calms the wind and sea by stretching out arms)
- Several disciples (pretend to row the boat, then act afraid and wake up Jesus)

Directions for Children
We can role-play the story of Jesus calming the storm. Role-playing means acting out the story as it is read from the bible. There are no lines to learn or say. You just do actions. This will help us become familiar with the story and remember it.

For this story, we need volunteers to play Jesus and several of his disciples. Who wants to participate?

This Gospel story has lots of action. How we can act the parts?

Listen carefully as the story is read to know what actions to do with the story.

Pray Together

Lord Jesus,

guide us to have faith in you even when life is difficult
and we're afraid and confused.
May we remember that you walk with us each day
through the difficult times and during the storms of life.
Give us hope to overcome our fear
and help us share our hope in you with others.
We place our trust in you, and we live now
and always as your followers. Amen.

Love God and Others

MATTHEW 22:34–39

GOD'S LOVE • LOVING OUR NEIGHBOR • SERVICE

When the Pharisees heard that he had silenced the Sadducees, they gathered together, and one of them [a scholar of the law] tested him by asking, "Teacher, which commandment in the law is the greatest?" He said to him, "You shall love the Lord, your God, with all your heart, with all your soul, and with all your mind. This is the greatest and the first commandment. The second is like it: You shall love your neighbor as yourself."

Introduce the Gospel Story

Who are people who love you? How do they show their love to you?

We love God because God created us and loves us without end. We are also called to love other people like we love God and like we love ourselves—and that's a lot of love! Our Gospel story today reminds us how important God's love is to each of us.

Share a Meditation

Close your eyes, listen to the Gospel story, and imagine yourself in the scene.

It's a beautiful day, and the sun is shining. You're outside with the crowd, listening to Jesus teach. You like listening to what Jesus has to say. He's unlike anyone you have ever heard.

You see one of the Pharisees come up to Jesus. He tries to trick Jesus with difficult questions. He asks Jesus, "Teacher, which commandment is the greatest?" You think that's a really tough question. You wonder what Jesus will say.

Jesus answers, "Love the Lord your God with all your heart. This is the first commandment." You think Jesus has it right. Loving God, who created us and loves us, is the most important thing we do. But Jesus is not finished. He continues, "And the second commandment is 'Love your neighbor.'"

You think of how Jesus lives this. He cures the sick and teaches the people day after day. Surely he gets tired! But he always seems to have time for those who need him. You realize Jesus has shown us by his actions how to love one another. Surely he comes from God!

You wonder how you can love as Jesus teaches. Ask Jesus for the help you need to love other people. Hear Jesus speaking to you in your heart.

Now open your eyes and come back to the group. Do any of you want to share what Jesus said to you?

Ask Questions

- *What does the Pharisee ask Jesus?*
- *What does Jesus answer?*
- *Why is it important to love God?*
- *How much are we to love others?*
- *What are ways we can show love to other people?*
- *How are we expected to help people in need?*
- *Should we pray for people we don't know?*

Reflect and Wrap Up the Discussion

God created us and made everything in our world for love of us. So many wonderful things God created for us! We must give thanks and praise to God for all God has done. We must remember that we love God because God first loved us.

Jesus also calls us to love other people, to be people of compassion who reach out to others. It's a challenge to care about people we don't even like, yet Jesus showed us by his life that this is what we are to do.

We're to live the greatest commandment in what we do each day. When we love God and love others, we're living as God created us to live.

Craft Activity

CREATE LIVE-IN-LOVE HEARTS

Materials

- Construction paper
- Scissors
- Markers

Directions for Children

We know that God calls us to live in love. Sometimes people think this just means being nice. But this Gospel can be a challenge to put into action.

Can you think of ways to live in love? Here are some ideas: read a story to a younger brother or sister, help an elderly person with a chore, donate a new toy to a shelter, pray for people who are poor.

1. Now cut out a heart from construction paper.
2. On your heart, write one way you will live in love. This should be something you will do this week.

Take your hearts home and tell your family about this project. Maybe other family members will want to do their own live-in-love hearts!

Pray Together

God of the universe,
we give you praise for all that you are
and all that you have done for us.
Thank you for your love for each one of us
and help us to share that love with others.
Open our eyes and our hearts to people in need.
May we witness to your love for all people
by the way we live each day. Amen.

From *Plant the Seed: Sharing the Gospel With Children* (Liguori Publications, © 2011 Patricia Mathson).

See Jesus in Others

MATTHEW 25:34–40

GOD'S LOVE • LOVING OUR NEIGHBOR • SERVICE

Then the king will say to those on his right, "Come, you who are blessed by my Father. Inherit the kingdom prepared for you from the foundation of the world. For I was hungry and you gave me food, I was thirsty and you gave me drink, a stranger and you welcomed me, naked and you clothed me, ill and you cared for me, in prison and you visited me." Then the righteous will answer him and say, "Lord, when did we see you hungry and feed you, or thirsty and give you drink? When did we see you a stranger and welcome you, or naked and clothe you? When did we see you ill or in prison, and visit you?" And the king will say to them in reply, "Amen, I say to you, whatever you did for one of these least brothers of mine, you did for me."

....

Introduce the Gospel Story

Have you ever been hungry? Would it be difficult to be hungry all the time?

In the Gospels, we see Jesus Christ as a compassionate and caring person who reaches out to the poor, the sick, and the outcasts. Jesus calls us to serve others just as he did. Jesus told this Gospel story for all of us.

Share a Meditation

Bow your head and close your eyes. Picture yourself in this story.

You are sitting in the shade of a tree. You are part of the crowd that has followed Jesus. He's been telling stories to the people and teaching them. You're not sure you understand some of the things Jesus says, but you know in your heart that he speaks the truth.

Jesus tells a story about a king who invites people into his kingdom. He invites those who have given him food and drink, welcomed him, clothed him, taken care of him when he was sick, and visited him in prison. The people ask the king when did they do these things for him. And the king replies that whenever they helped people in need, they helped him too.

You begin to understand that the king in this story is Jesus. He's calling you to see him in other people. Jesus always takes time for people who come to him for help. You realize that Jesus is calling on us all to show mercy and kindness to others as if the person in need was Jesus himself.

You think about what you can do to serve others. How can you help people in need? Then you see Jesus make his way through the crowd and come over to you. He sits beside you and smiles at you. What does Jesus say to you? What do you say to Jesus?

Open your eyes now as we talk about this Gospel story. Do any of you want to share what you said to Jesus?

Ask Questions

* *Whom did the king invite into his kingdom?*
* *What does it mean to see Jesus in others?*
* *How can we help people who are hungry?*
* *What are ways to care for people who are sick, in the hospital, or homebound?*
* *How can we share what we have with others?*

Reflect and Wrap Up the Discussion

Jesus Christ teaches us that we are to see him in other people. We should have compassion for others and serve them as if we were serving Jesus himself.

Many people live in difficult circumstances. We must share what we have so that others may have what they need to live. With God's help, we can help others one person at a time. Each of us must work for justice for all people. This means that we are to help bring about the kingdom of God.

Service Activity

SHARE WITH CHILDREN IN THE HOSPITAL

Materials
* Paper or cardboard for making posters
* Markers
* Large collection boxes

Adult Preparation

1. Announce service project to children's families, other friends and family members, and the parish community.
2. Prepare collection boxes and secure locations to collect items.

Directions for Children

We can help others as Jesus Christ teaches us by doing a project for sick children in the hospital. These children sometimes must have many tests and treatments to get well.

We're going to collect new toys for the children's hospital. That way, children will be able to select a toy after their treatment to help them think about something else.

Today we're going to make signs and posters advertising our toy collection. Each of you can help decorate a sign asking people to help sick children, because that is what Jesus wants us to do.

Let your families know about this project. Remember that all toys have to be new, because they are going to sick children. We're all called to have compassion for other people. With God's help, we can bring joy to sick children.

Pray Together

Lord Jesus Christ,
we know that you call us to see your presence in each person.
Help us look beyond our own wants to the needs of others.
Enable us to live the challenge of the Gospel.
Open our hearts to the hungry, the sick, and those in need.
Empower us to make each day a time of reaching out to others.
May we remember that what we do for others we do for you.
Amen.

From *Plant the Seed: Sharing the Gospel With Children* (Liguori Publications, © 2011 Patricia Mathson). Permission to reproduce granted to original purchaser for noncommercial use only.

Prayer in the Garden

MATTHEW 26:36–45

HOLY WEEK • PRAYER • FOLLOWING JESUS

Then Jesus came with them to a place called Gethsemane, and he said to his disciples, "Sit here while I go over there and pray." He took along Peter and the two sons of Zebedee, and began to feel sorrow and distress. Then he said to them, "My soul is sorrowful even to death. Remain here and keep watch with me." He advanced a little and fell prostrate in prayer, saying, "My Father, if it is possible, let this cup pass from me; yet, not as I will, but as you will." When he returned to his disciples he found them asleep. He said to Peter, "So you could not keep watch with me for one hour? Watch and pray that you may not undergo the test. The spirit is willing, but the flesh is weak." Withdrawing a second time, he prayed again, "My Father, if it is not possible that this cup pass without my drinking it, your will be done!" Then he returned once more and found them asleep, for they could not keep their eyes open. He left them and withdrew again and prayed a third time, saying the same thing again. Then he returned to his disciples and said to them, "Are you still sleeping and taking your rest? Behold, the hour is at hand when the Son of Man is to be handed over to sinners."

....

Introduce the Gospel Story

Do you pray when life is difficult? How does prayer help us?

On the night before he died, Jesus went into the garden and prayed to the Father. He knew he was facing death on a cross for us. Our story today is about that night. We remember that we should be people of prayer like Jesus. Prayer is important in our relationship with God.

Share a Meditation

Close your eyes and put aside all other thoughts. See yourself with Jesus and the disciples in the garden after the Last Supper.

You see Jesus come into the garden with some of his disciples. You wonder why Jesus has come here this night.

You see Jesus turn to his disciples and hear him tell them his heart is full of sorrow. Then he says, "Sit here while I go over there and pray." Jesus walks a short distance and begins to pray. You're close enough to hear the prayer of Jesus. He says, "My Father, if it is possible, let this suffering pass from me! But I am not asking what I want, but what you want." You hear Jesus' voice break. You wonder what is going on.

Jesus goes back to the disciples. They're not praying, but are sound asleep. Jesus stands in front of Peter and says, "Could you not stay awake for one hour?" Jesus goes back to where he was praying. Again he returns and finds the disciples asleep. You wonder how they can sleep when something is wrong. Jesus goes off to pray, comes back a third time, and finds them fast asleep. He asks them, "How can you be sleeping now? The time is coming where I will be handed over to sinners." You know that right now, Jesus needs his friends to pray for him and to stay awake.

You think back to when you could have prayed, but you were too busy, too tired, or had other things to do. Tell Jesus from your heart how you will make more time for prayer in your life. Hear him answer you.

Then open your eyes. Do any of you want to share how you will make more time to pray?

Ask Questions

- > *In this Gospel story, where did Jesus and his disciples go?*
- > *What did the disciples do while Jesus was praying?*
- > *What did Jesus say to them?*
- > *How can we put Jesus first?*
- > *Why is prayer important for everyone?*
- > *What are ways we can pray to God?*
- > *How often should we pray?*

Reflect and Wrap Up the Discussion

Prayer is an important part of our relationship with God. Prayer helps us talk to God and to make sense of our lives and who we are as followers of Jesus Christ.

We should pray from our hearts. We should take time for prayer. We should pray like Jesus did and not like the disciples did that night.

Prayer connects us not only with God, but with one another as a community of God's people who must pray for others' needs as well as our own. In all that we do and all that we are, we must be people of prayer.

Craft Activity

USE PRAYER WORDS

Materials

- Writing paper
- Pens or pencils
- Markers, crayons, or colored pencils

Directions for Children

We can pray in many different ways. We can give thanks. We can ask for help for ourselves or for others. We can pray alone. We can pray with others. We can pray with the words of traditional prayers. We can pray in our own words.

One way to pray in our own words is to learn to use prayer words. Here is a list of words on which to center prayer: peace, making good choices, compassion, the future, joy, gratitude, justice, and hope. There are many other prayer words too.

1. Choose a prayer word and write a short prayer on that topic. Your prayer can be one sentence or one paragraph.
2. Decorate your prayer.

Those who choose to can share their prayers with the group. This helps us learn from the ideas of others.

Pray Together

Lord and Savior,
we ask you to help us follow your example
and be people of prayer in all times and places.
May we never be too busy to turn to you in prayer.
Open our hearts to your love and your presence with us
so we may weave prayer into all we do.
In this way may we give glory to you each day
by our words and our actions. Amen.

From *Plant the Seed: Sharing the Gospel With Children* (Liguori Publications, © 2011 Patricia Mathson). Permission to reproduce granted to original purchaser for noncommercial use only.

Share the Good News

MATTHEW 28:1–10

EASTER • FOLLOWING JESUS • GOD'S LOVE • NEW LIFE

After the sabbath, as the first day of the week was dawning, Mary Magdalene and the other Mary came to see the tomb. And behold, there was a great earthquake; for an angel of the Lord descended from heaven, approached, rolled back the stone, and sat upon it. His appearance was like lightning and his clothing was white as snow. The guards were shaken with fear of him and became like dead men. Then the angel said to the women in reply, "Do not be afraid! I know that you are seeking Jesus the crucified. He is not here, for he has been raised just as he said. Come and see the place where he lay. Then go quickly and tell his disciples, 'He has been raised from the dead, and he is going before you to Galilee; there you will see him.' Behold, I have told you." Then they went away quickly from the tomb, fearful yet overjoyed, and ran to announce this to his disciples. And behold, Jesus met them on their way and greeted them. They approached, embraced his feet, and did him homage. Then Jesus said to them, "Do not be afraid. Go tell my brothers to go to Galilee, and there they will see me."

. . . .

Introduce the Gospel Story

Did something exciting ever happen to you? Did you tell other people about it?

In this story, we'll hear Jesus talk about sharing his Good News. We know Jesus came for everyone, and he'll help us share his story with everyone we meet. Jesus is with us always.

Share a Meditation

Close your eyes and imagine this scene.

It's the Sunday after Jesus died on a cross. You're with Mary Magdalene and another woman named Mary as they go to the tomb where Jesus' body had been placed. It's quiet as you walk along. You think over the events of the past few days and cannot believe all that has happened.

All of a sudden, the ground begins to shake. You wonder what is happening. Is it an earthquake? You look toward the tomb and see that the big rock that was at the entrance has been rolled away. On top of it sits an angel. What can this mean?

The angel says, "Don't be afraid. I know you're looking for Jesus. He's not here. He has risen as he said."

You wonder if this can really be true.

Then the angel says, "Go and tell the disciples that Jesus is going to Galilee." You dare to hope for the first time in days.

You go with Mary Magdalene and the other Mary to tell the disciples the Good News. On the way, you see someone in the distance. As you get closer, you see it's Jesus! He smiles. "Go and tell my disciples to go to Galilee," he tells Mary Magdalene, "and there they will see me." You think what a wonderful day this is. Jesus is alive! You can't wait to tell everyone you see.

Now feel the presence and love of the risen Christ. Talk to Jesus in your own words. What do you say to him? What does Jesus say to you?

Now open your eyes and know that Jesus is here with us always. Would any of you like to share what Jesus said to you?

Ask Questions

- ❧ Where were the women going?
- ❧ What happened on the way to the tomb?
- ❧ What did the angel by the tomb tell them?
- ❧ Whom did the women see on the way to tell the disciples?
- ❧ What did Jesus ask them to do?
- ❧ How can we share the Good News with others?
- ❧ Do we teach about Jesus with words or actions?

Reflect and Wrap Up the Discussion

We are all called by our baptism to share the Good News of Jesus Christ. Faith in Jesus Christ and his Good News should transform our hearts and lives. Each of us has a story of faith to share with others.

We share the Good News by our words and our actions. Without actions, our words have no meaning. We're people who can't wait to share the Word of God! As we share God's Word, our own faith in God is renewed. We're all called to live this Gospel.

Craft Activity

MAKE NEW-LIFE CROSSES
Materials
- Images of flowers and foliage from garden catalogs or magazines
- Scissors
- Glue sticks
- Construction paper

Adult Preparation
Cut images of flowers or foliage from garden catalogs or other magazines for children to choose from.

Directions for Children
We're going to make new-life crosses to help us remember that Jesus brings new life to all of us. The cross of Good Friday has no meaning without the resurrection of Easter Sunday. Jesus redeemed us by his life, death, and resurrection.

1. Select a picture of flowers or other plants. Cut this picture into the shape of a cross.
2. Glue the flowered cross to a piece of construction paper.
3. Next, cut a larger cross shape in the construction paper around the smaller cross. This makes a border of color around the flowered cross.

These colorful crosses remind us of the new life Jesus brings us.

Pray Together

Lord Jesus Christ,
we give you praise for all you have done for us
through your life, death, and resurrection.
Give us the courage to follow your way of love
in all we do and say each day.
May we share the Good News
so others can hear the message of love of the Gospel
and come to know you. Amen.

From *Plant the Seed: Sharing the Gospel With Children* (Liguori Publications, © 2011 Patricia Mathson). Permission to reproduce granted to original purchaser for noncommercial use only.

CHAPTER 2

Sharing the Gospel of Mark

Share Background With Students

In the Gospel of Mark, we experience the story of Jesus' ministry to the people. He tells parables to help his followers understand the Word of God. He proclaims God's love for all people to the crowds who follow him. This Gospel shows us what it means to be a disciple. As Jesus walks from Galilee to Jerusalem, we walk with him.

We see how Jesus teaches his followers by his words *and* by his actions. We see Jesus as a person of compassion for others. He heals the blind and the lame. We see that the miracles are not just for the people Jesus cures—those miracles are also signs for the community to show that Jesus is from God, as he says he is.

Jesus came for all people. He shares God's love with all who listen to him. He loves each of us, even those who are difficult to love. He loves children and calls them to come to him. We too are called to have compassion for the sick, the outcasts, and others in need. This Gospel calls us to live the Good News.

The way won't be easy. We're to pick up our crosses and follow Jesus—even to his death on a cross. But this is the path to the new life Jesus Christ brings to all of us. We're called through this Gospel to be faithful to God as God is always faithful to us. In this way, we live as disciples of Jesus Christ in all we say and do.

Jesus Cures the Sick

MARK 1:40–45

HEALING • LOVING OUR NEIGHBOR • SERVICE

A leper came to him (and kneeling down) begged him and said, "If you wish, you can make me clean." Moved with pity, he stretched out his hand, touched him, and said to him, "I do will it. Be made clean." The leprosy left him immediately, and he was made clean. Then, warning him sternly, he dismissed him at once. Then he said to him, "See that you tell no one anything, but go, show yourself to the priest and offer for your cleansing what Moses prescribed; that will be proof for them." The man went away and began to publicize the whole matter. He spread the report abroad so that it was impossible for Jesus to enter a town openly. He remained outside in deserted places, and people kept coming to him from everywhere.

. . . .

Introduce the Gospel Story

Have you ever been sick? How did you feel? Did other people help you?

We're going to hear a story about Jesus healing a man with a skin disease called *leprosy*. It was so feared that people with leprosy had to stay away from others for the rest of their lives.

Share a Meditation

Close your eyes. Imagine you're living in the time of Jesus.

You are in the crowd following Jesus in Galilee. You think Jesus is really a great teacher. He helps you look at things in a different way.

A person with leprosy comes up to Jesus. You know that people like this aren't supposed to come near other people. Surely Jesus will send the man away! But the man comes and kneels in front of Jesus. You hear the man say, "If you choose, you can make me clean." Wow, you think, that man really has faith in Jesus.

You watch as Jesus reaches out and puts his hand on the man's shoulder. You wonder how he can touch that man. Jesus says to the man with leprosy, "Be made clean." You look at the man and can't believe your eyes. All the sores on his skin are healed! How can that be? Truly Jesus is God.

Then Jesus tells the man to go and show himself to the priest so he can go back to his family. The man is so happy! He tells everyone he sees about what happened to him.

You can hardly believe what you saw!

You think about what Jesus has been saying about loving others. You look over to where Jesus is, and he looks back at you. You know Jesus wants you to care about other people. Are there people you think of as outcasts? How can you help them?

When you're ready, open your eyes. Would any of you like to tell us how you think we can help others?

Ask Questions

- In this Gospel story, what did the man with leprosy say to Jesus?
- Why do you think Jesus cured the man with leprosy?
- Why could Jesus work miracles?
- What are ways to help people who are sick at home or in the hospital?

Reflect and Wrap Up the Discussion

The Gospels are filled with stories of Jesus' compassion for people who were sick. In this story, a man had faith in Jesus and was healed. He was no longer an outcast, and he could go home to his family and friends. Meeting Jesus changed his life.

We sometimes treat people like outcasts. Let's look into our hearts and see whom we ignore or look down on. We are to follow the example of love of Jesus Christ. His life shows us that each person must be treated with respect as part of God's family.

Service Activity

MAKE GET-WELL CARDS

Materials

- Construction paper
- Scrapbook paper
- Scissors
- Glue sticks
- Markers, crayons, or colored pencils

Directions for Children

We should follow the example of Jesus in caring about the sick. One way to do this is by making beautiful get-well cards for people who are ill.

We've all been sick, and we know how hard that can be. It seems to help us if we know other people care. So let's make cards for people in our parish who are sick or in the hospital.

1. Choose a sheet of construction paper and fold it in half to make a card.
2. Cut shapes from colorful scrapbook paper.
3. Glue the shapes to the front of the card.
4. Inside the card, write a cheery greeting such as "Get Well Soon!" or "Thinking of You." Then sign your first name.

People who are sick will appreciate your kind gesture.

Pray Together

Lord Jesus Christ,
we thank you for your love for all people
and the example you showed of caring about the sick.
May those who struggle with illness know the comfort
of your presence and love.
Open our hearts to people who are in the hospital,
in care centers, undergoing treatment, or sick at home.
May we find ways to show compassion to others
as you showed us by your example. Amen.

From *Plant the Seed: Sharing the Gospel With Children* (Liguori Publications, © 2011 Patricia Mathson). Permission to reproduce granted to original purchaser for noncommercial use only.

Lame Man Walks Again

MARK 2:2–12

FRIENDSHIP • HEALING • LOVING OUR NEIGHBOR • SERVICE

Many gathered together so that there was no longer room for them, not even around the door, and he preached the word to them. They came bringing to him a paralytic carried by four men. Unable to get near Jesus because of the crowd, they opened up the roof above him. After they had broken through, they let down the mat on which the paralytic was lying. When Jesus saw their faith, he said to the paralytic, "Child, your sins are forgiven." Now some of the scribes were sitting there asking themselves, "Why does this man speak that way? He is blaspheming. Who but God alone can forgive sins?"

Jesus immediately knew in his mind what they were thinking to them-selves, so he said, "Why are you thinking such things in your hearts? Which is easier, to say to the paralytic, 'Your sins are forgiven,' or to say, 'Rise, pick up your mat and walk'? But that you may know that the Son of Man has authority to forgive sins on earth"—he said to the paralytic, "I say to you, rise, pick up your mat, and go home." He rose, picked up his mat at once, and went away in the sight of everyone. They were all astounded and glorified God, saying, "We have never seen anything like this."

Introduce the Gospel Story

Do your friends ever help you? What do they do for you? Do they help you with things you can't do by yourself?

Friends are important. This Gospel meditation is about how a man's friends helped him get to Jesus. He couldn't walk, so his friends were determined to take him to Jesus to be healed. There was such a crowd, they had to go through the roof of the house! Then Jesus cured the man, and he could walk again.

Share a Meditation

Close your eyes. See yourself in this Gospel story.

You are listening to Jesus teach in a crowded house. You look out the door and see that so many people have come to hear Jesus that not everyone can come inside.

A man is being carried on a mat by four people because he cannot walk. But they cannot get through the crowd to the door. Then you hear noise on the top of the house and look up. They've made a hole in the roof and are lowering the man on a mat.

Jesus says to the man, "Your sins are forgiven." You hear muttering among the scribes sitting near you: "What does he think he's doing? Only God can forgive sins." The scribes have heard Jesus teach and have seen his miracles, but they didn't open their hearts to who Jesus really was.

Then Jesus says to the man, "Get up, take your mat, and go on home." The man slowly stands. He can walk! This will change his life! The man picks up his mat and walks out the door. The crowd outside the door moves aside as the man leaves. Suddenly everyone begins to talk. They give glory to God. What a wonderful thing Jesus has done!

Talk to Jesus now in the silence of your heart. Give thanks to Jesus for all he has done for you. Listen to what Jesus says to you.

Open your eyes now. Can you share what Jesus has done for you?

Ask Questions

- *Why were the four people carrying their friend on the mat?*
- *Why couldn't they get in the door?*
- *What did Jesus tell the lame man?*
- *Why did the scribes mutter to each other?*
- *What did the lame man do?*
- *Did everyone believe in Jesus?*
- *Why could Jesus heal people?*

Reflect and Wrap Up the Discussion

In this Gospel story, we witness a miracle of Jesus. He forgives a person's sins. He cures the lame man as proof to the people. We too can experience God's mercy and forgiveness. We only have to go to Jesus.

This Gospel is another example of Jesus serving others. We're called to follow in his footsteps. We may not be able to do all Jesus did, but we can make a difference in others' lives, one person at a time.

Service Activity

HELP THE SICK

Materials

- Writing paper
- Pens or pencils

Directions for Children

We can follow Jesus' example in caring about people who are sick. Let's make a list of ways we can help the sick:

- Bring homework to a sick classmate
- Make a gift basket with items for a homebound elderly person
- Prepare food for families with children in hospital
- Lend a favorite book to a sick friend who has to stay inside
- Do yard work for someone who is in the hospital
- Donate to an organization that helps sick children around the world

This list shows us practical ways to help people who are sick. What are some other ideas? Try to use one of your service ideas this week.

Pray Together

Jesus, Savior and Teacher,

you showed you are God by your words and your miracles.

You healed a lame man so he could walk,

but still people didn't believe, because their hearts were not open.

Help us see your power at work each day,

and may we have faith in you at all times and places. Amen.

From *Plant the Seed: Sharing the Gospel With Children* (Liguori Publications, © 2011 Patricia Mathson). Permission to reproduce granted to original purchaser for noncommercial use only.

Sower Plants the Seed

MARK 4:3–8, 13–20

WORD OF GOD • GOD'S LOVE • SIN

Hear this! A sower went out to sow. And as he sowed, some seed fell on the path, and the birds came and ate it up. Other seed fell on rocky ground where it had little soil. It sprang up at once because the soil was not deep. And when the sun rose, it was scorched and it withered for lack of roots. Some seed fell among thorns, and the thorns grew up and choked it and it produced no grain. And some seed fell on rich soil and produced fruit. It came up and grew and yielded thirty, sixty, and a hundredfold.

Do you not understand this parable? Then how will you understand any of the parables? The sower sows the word. These are the ones on the path where the word is sown. As soon as they hear, Satan comes at once and takes away the word sown in them. And these are the ones sown on rocky ground who, when they hear the word, receive it at once with joy. But they have no root; they last only for a time. Then when tribulation or persecution comes because of the word, they quickly fall away. Those sown among thorns are another sort. They are the people who hear the word, but worldly anxiety, the lure of riches, and the craving for other things intrude and choke the word, and it bears no fruit. But those sown on rich soil are the ones who hear the word and accept it and bear fruit thirty and sixty and a hundredfold.

Introduce the Gospel Story

Did you ever plant a garden? Did you water and take care of it?

As followers of Jesus Christ, we're to hear the Word of God and live it. This Gospel reminds us to let the Word of God grow in our hearts. We mustn't let other things or other people lead us away from God. Only in God can we become who we were created to be.

Share a Meditation

Breathe deeply in and out. Feel yourself relax. Now put yourself in this Gospel story.

You're in the crowd of people by the sea listening to Jesus tell the story of a person who goes out to plant seed in a field. Some of the seed fell on rocky ground. It could grow only shallow roots and soon died. Some seed ended up among thorns that choked it as it grew. And some seed fell on rich soil and produced many plants.

You're happy when Jesus says he'll explain the meaning of this story. He says the seed is the Word of God in people's lives. Some people listen to the Word, but when hard times come, they turn away from God. They forget that God loves us and is always with us in the good times and the bad times.

Jesus explains that other people hear the Word, but it is choked out by their desire for riches and power. People often focus on things that aren't important. Jesus ends his explanation by talking about people who hear the Word of God and accept it, and it grows in their hearts.

You know Jesus is speaking to you. Talk now to Jesus in your heart. Ask him how to live the Word of God. What does he say to you?

Now come back as we gather again. Do any of you want to share what Jesus said to you?

Ask Questions

- In this Gospel story, what is the seed?
- What are ways we hear the Word of God?
- What keep us from growing in faith?
- Is it easy to have faith when times are tough?
- How can we grow in faith?
- How can we live God's Word?
- How can we share God's Word with others?

Reflect and Wrap Up the Discussion

The parable of the sower is a story for all of us. Jesus told parables to help people understand their faith in God. The parables used experiences from the lives of his listeners. This scene would have been familiar to the people of his time.

In this story, the seed is the Word of God. We are reminded to have faith in God in difficult times. We must let the Word of God grow in our hearts. We shouldn't let other things distract us. The words of the Gospels speak to us today as they did to the people who first heard them in the time of Jesus.

Prayer Activity

LOOK UP GOSPEL VERSES
Materials
- Bibles

Directions for Children
We can learn about God's Word by looking up verses from the four Gospels. We can discuss what each of these verses means to us today.

- I am with you always (Matthew 28:20).
- All things are possible for God (Mark 10:27).
- Forgive and you will be forgiven (Luke 6:37).
- I am the way and the truth and the life (John 14:6).
- Whoever loves me will keep my word (John 14:23).

As we read these words, let's allow Jesus' teachings to grow in our hearts. These and other Gospel verses help us live as followers of Jesus Christ. To live the Word of God, we must know it.

Pray Together

Lord Jesus Christ,
help us be open to your Word
that it may grow in our hearts
and become part of who we are.
May we live what we believe
in all we do each day.
Help us grow in faith in you,
hope in the future,
and love for you and for other people. Amen.

Let the Children Come

MARK 10:13–16

FOLLOWING JESUS • GOD'S LOVE • PRAYER

And people were bringing children to him that he might touch them, but the disciples rebuked them. When Jesus saw this he became indignant and said to them, "Let the children come to me; do not prevent them, for the kingdom of God belongs to such as these. Amen, I say to you, whoever does not accept the kingdom of God like a child will not enter it." Then he embraced them and blessed them, placing his hands on them.

Introduce the Gospel Story

Do people ever tell you to go away because they're busy? How does that make you feel?

We're going to share a Gospel story about how Jesus loves children. This story reminds us that Jesus is never too busy to spend time with us. He came for people of all ages, cultures, and nations. He loves the old and young, the rich and the poor. Jesus came for everyone.

Share a Meditation

Now let us quiet ourselves and picture this Gospel story in our minds.

Imagine that you're there that day in the crowd following Jesus. His words have touched your heart.

A group of children go to where Jesus is sitting. You see the smiles on the faces of the children as they approach Jesus. Then some of Jesus' disciples stop the children. They say Jesus is too busy for them. The children look sad. Then Jesus tells the disciples, "Let the children come to me." The disciples step aside, and the children go up to Jesus.

You hear Jesus talking to the children. They're laughing and talking excitedly. Jesus is smiling as he listens to what the children have to say. You see him bless the children. You want to go over and talk to Jesus, too, but you aren't sure what to do.

Then Jesus calls you over. You sit next to him. Jesus smiles. What does Jesus say to you? What do you say to Jesus?

Now open your eyes. Do any of you want to share what Jesus said to you?

Ask Questions

- *In this Gospel story, where were the children going?*
- *What did the disciples do?*
- *What did Jesus say to the disciples?*
- *Is Jesus ever too busy to listen to us?*
- *Does Jesus love all children?*

Reflect and Wrap Up the Discussion

This Gospel story shows us how much Jesus loves children. This is a story for you today as much as it was for the children who saw Jesus that day. Jesus loves each of you and calls you to be with him.

We can talk to Jesus any time in prayer. Jesus will always hear us, because Jesus is always with us. He listens to our prayers and cares about us. Through prayer, we stay connected with Jesus.

Share the love of Jesus with another child this week. Make the message of this Gospel story part of your lives.

Craft Activity

DRAW GOSPEL PICTURES
Materials
- Drawing paper
- Construction paper
- Markers, crayons, or colored pencils
- Scissors
- Glue sticks

Directions for Children
God gives us the ability to draw and create works of art. Let's make pictures of the Gospel story of Jesus and the children to help us remember this story. We'll have to use our imaginations!

1. Draw Jesus in the picture along with some children. Be sure to include yourself in the picture.
2. At the bottom of the picture print "Jesus loves the children," which is the message of this Gospel story.
3. When you're finished, cut around the edge of the paper with scissors in a wavy pattern to make a fancy edge.
4. Use a glue stick to attach the picture to a larger sheet of construction paper. This frames the picture and gives the artwork a finished look.

Remember: Jesus will always love you!

Pray Together

Lord Jesus Christ,
we know you care about
children of all ages and all nations,
all races and all religions.
Open our hearts and our lives
to the needs of children
in our communities and our world.
Help us follow your example
by never being too busy to welcome
a child in your holy name.
May children everywhere come to know
your love and care. Amen.

From *Plant the Seed: Sharing the Gospel With Children* (Liguori Publications, © 2011 Patricia Mathson). Permission to reproduce granted to original purchaser for noncommercial use only.

Rich Man Walks Away

MARK 10:17–22

FOLLOWING JESUS • LOVING OUR NEIGHBOR
SELFISHNESS • SERVICE

As he was setting out on a journey, a man ran up, knelt down before him, and asked him, "Good teacher, what must I do to inherit eternal life?" Jesus answered him, "Why do you call me good? No one is good but God alone. You know the commandments: 'You shall not kill; you shall not commit adultery; you shall not steal; you shall not bear false witness; you shall not defraud; honor your father and your mother.'" He replied and said to him, "Teacher, all of these I have observed from my youth." Jesus, looking at him, loved him and said to him, "You are lacking in one thing. Go, sell what you have, and give to (the) poor and you will have treasure in heaven; then come, follow me." At that statement his face fell, and he went away sad, for he had many possessions.

Introduce the Gospel Story

Do you like your toys, games, and clothes? Do you think possessions are more important than people?

We're going to share a meditation about a rich young man who seemed to have everything. But he had a difficult time sharing his possessions. He tried to fill up the empty place in his heart with a lot of things. But what was missing was caring about other people.

Share a Meditation

Close your eyes and listen carefully. Put yourself in this story from the Gospels.

As Jesus is walking along the road, you're in the crowd following him. Another person comes up to Jesus. You recognize the person as a rich man from a nearby town.

The rich man asks Jesus how to gain eternal life. Jesus smiles at the rich man and says, "You lack one thing. Sell what you own and give the money to the poor. Then come, follow me." The rich man looks at Jesus and walks away. He is sad because he didn't want to give up anything he owned. Jesus looks at the man as he leaves, and his heart is full of sorrow.

You think about what just happened. How can the rich man just ignore what Jesus said? Then you realize that you too have many possessions you really like and that would be difficult to give up. You realize we each need to help others. We who have much must reach out to those who have less.

You understand that you need to make some choices. You need to open your heart to others' needs. Ask Jesus to help you think of ways to serve others. He'll always have time to listen to you. Hear him speak to you.

Open your eyes. Do any of you want to share what Jesus told you?

Ask Questions

- In this Gospel story, what did the rich young man ask Jesus?
- What did Jesus say the rich young man needed to do?
- Why did the young man go away?
- What does Jesus want us to do?
- Is it easy to follow Jesus?
- How did Jesus treat people who were poor?
- How can we share what we have with people in need?

Reflect and Wrap Up the Discussion

In this story, the rich man's possessions became the most important thing in his life. He walked away from Jesus. Sometimes we do the same thing. We may find ourselves thinking more about what we want than about how to serve God. This keeps us from putting Jesus first.

Let's see in this story how we are to live as followers of Jesus Christ. We're all given the resources of the Earth to share with others. Jesus showed that we're called to serve people who are poor and in need.

Service Activity

ASSEMBLE WELCOME BAGS

Materials
- Gift bags (not trash bags)

Adult Preparation
1. Ask a shelter which items they need most.
2. Ask children to bring those items to class.

Directions for Children

Sometimes children and families must stay at a shelter because they have nowhere else to go. This can be an uncertain time in children's lives.

We're going to put together welcome bags for children as they arrive at the family shelter.

We will assemble the welcome bags together. Make sure each bag has a toy and some personal-care items.

The bags will be delivered to the shelter to help children at a time when they need it most. Thank you for reaching out to children in need!

Pray Together

Lord, Teacher and Redeemer,
help us live the message of the Gospel
and share our time, talent, and treasure
with people who are hurting and in need.
May we realize what is important
and give to others in your name.
Teach us your way, that we may give glory
to you by the way we share. Amen.

From *Plant the Seed: Sharing the Gospel With Children* (Liguori Publications, © 2011 Patricia Mathson). Permission to reproduce granted to original purchaser for noncommercial use only.

Blind Man Sees Jesus

MARK 10:46–52

FAITH • GOD'S LOVE • HEALING

They came to Jericho. And as he was leaving Jericho with his disciples and a sizable crowd, Bartimaeus, a blind man, the son of Timaeus, sat by the roadside begging. On hearing that it was Jesus of Nazareth, he began to cry out and say, "Jesus, son of David, have pity on me." And many rebuked him, telling him to be silent. But he kept calling out all the more, "Son of David, have pity on me." Jesus stopped and said, "Call him." So they called the blind man, saying to him, "Take courage; get up, he is calling you." He threw aside his cloak, sprang up, and came to Jesus. Jesus said to him in reply, "What do you want me to do for you?" The blind man replied to him, "Master, I want to see." Jesus told him, "Go your way; your faith has saved you." Immediately he received his sight and followed him on the way.

Introduce the Gospel Story

What do you think it would be like to be blind? What are some things you wouldn't be able to see?

This Gospel is about a blind man who wanted to see. He had faith, so Jesus cured the blind man and he could see again. This story shows us that Jesus cares about all people. He loves us with an unending love. We see in this Gospel story a glimpse of how our world was intended to be—without blindness and illness.

Share a Meditation

Bow your head or close your eyes. Put yourself in this story.

It's a cool day in Jericho, and you're in the crowd following Jesus. Suddenly you hear someone shout, "Jesus, have mercy on me!" You recognize the man. His name is Bartimaeus, the blind man who sits on the corner and begs for money.

Some people tell the man to be quiet and leave Jesus alone. But the man calls out again, and Jesus tells his disciples to call the man over. The disciples tell the blind man to get up because Jesus is calling him. They take the blind man to Jesus. You move in closer to see what happens next.

Jesus asks the blind man, "What do you what me to do for you?" The man says, "Let me see again." Jesus tells Bartimaeus, "Go, your faith has made you well." All of a sudden, the man can see. You can't believe it. How could this happen? Then you realize Jesus could do this only if he's God!

The crowd starts to move on, and you go also. The blind man joins the group following Jesus. You think you should have faith in Jesus, just as the blind man did. You've learned something important today. You know in your heart that Jesus is the Messiah. Give thanks now to God for God's unending love for you. Ask God for help to live in faith like the blind man.

Open your eyes and come back to this room and this time. Do any of you want to share an example of God's unending love?

Ask Questions

- Who called to Jesus?
- What did the blind man want?
- Did the blind man believe in Jesus?
- What did the blind man do after he could see?
- How do we see Jesus and his love for us?
- How are we called to live as followers of Jesus Christ?

Reflect and Wrap Up the Discussion

Jesus calls us to faith in God. In this story, the blind man didn't let the crowd's opinion silence him. We shouldn't let what other people think keep us from doing what is right.

The blind man could see who Jesus was. Other people, who had their sight, couldn't. Sometimes we're blind to God's presence in our lives. The blind man's encounter with Jesus leads him to follow Jesus. We too are called to walk in Jesus' footsteps and follow where he leads us.

Prayer Activity

SHARE FAITH PICTURES
Materials
- Magazines, calendars, or other sources of images
- Scissors

Adult Preparation
Cut pictures of people, animals, and nature from magazines.

Directions for Children
We can look at pictures and see how they speak to us of our faith in God. Select one of the pictures of people, animals, or nature that reminds you of God's presence in your life.

For example, a picture of a mountain may remind you that God created our world. A picture of an elderly person could represent the love your grandmother shows you. A picture of two chairs in a garden might remind you that God waits for us to come to him in prayer.

We can all share why we selected our pictures. We can grow and learn from one another's faith.

Pray Together

Lord Jesus Christ,
we know you healed a blind man
who had faith in you, and he followed you.
Open our eyes and our hearts to your presence
in the world and in the people around us.
Help us have faith in you at all times
and know that you are here with us each day.
May we recognize you in our lives
and follow you as the blind man did. Amen.

Widow Gives to Others

MARK 12:41–44

SERVICE • GOD'S LOVE
LOVING OUR NEIGHBOR • GENEROSITY

He sat down opposite the treasury and observed how the crowd put money into the treasury. Many rich people put in large sums. A poor widow also came and put in two small coins worth a few cents. Calling his disciples to himself, he said to them, "Amen, I say to you, this poor widow put in more than all the other contributors to the treasury. For they have all contributed from their surplus wealth, but she, from her poverty, has contributed all she had, her whole livelihood."

. . . .

Introduce the Gospel Story

Did you ever give money to help others? Is it easy to give away what we have?

This Gospel story is about someone who gave to the poor even though she didn't have much money. Jesus tells his followers that this woman gave from her heart. We should follow her example by sharing what we have.

Share a Meditation

Imagine you are with Jesus and his followers in Jerusalem.

You're in the temple area with Jesus and a group of his disciples. Everyone is gathered around Jesus to hear what he has to say. You're also watching the people as they go about their day. A few people put money in the offering box.

An older lady comes into the temple. She is your neighbor, a widow who is very poor. She puts two coins in the offering box. You hear the noise of the coins as they hit the bottom.

Jesus looks up, sees the woman, and says to his disciples, "I tell you that this poor widow has put in more than all the others." You wonder what he's talking about. Then Jesus explains that everyone else gave only what they didn't need, but she gave everything she had.

You realize Jesus is trying to teach something important: We're all called to give to others. We're to give from the bottom of our hearts so others will have what they need. Then Jesus turns to you. Listen to Jesus speaking in your heart. Tell Jesus how you'll share what you've been given.

Now open your eyes and rejoin our group. Can any of you tell us how you will share what you've been given?

Ask Questions

- *Where was Jesus teaching?*
- *Who put money in the offering box?*
- *How much did the widow put in?*
- *What did Jesus tell the disciples about the widow's offering?*
- *Why are we to share what we have with people who have less?*

Reflect and Wrap Up the Discussion

Jesus taught his followers the importance of giving to others. In this story, Jesus praises the widow who gave only a small donation to the temple because she gave most of what she had. She gave from her heart. Jesus challenges us to be like the widow. She's a model of faith for all of us.

Jesus often challenges us in the Gospels. Before this day, probably none of the disciples would have thought of a poor widow as someone who was an example for them. We can all learn about faith in God from unlikely people.

Service Activity

BE THERE FOR OTHERS
Directions for Children
Jesus calls us to look beyond our own needs and wants to the needs of others. Let's share some ways other people have helped us or someone we know.

This week, look for a way to help someone else, even in a small way. Many people need a kind word or someone to listen to them. We can be there for people when they need help. In this way, we build the kingdom of God one caring gesture at a time.

Pray Together

Dear Jesus,
we hear in the Gospel the story of the widow
who put only a few pennies in the temple collection.
She gave from her heart and gave most of what she had.
Help us learn to be generous from her example.
Open our hearts and our lives to the needs of others,
that we may help people in your name. Amen.

CHAPTER 3

Sharing the Gospel of Luke

Share Background With Students

In the Gospel of Luke, we see that Jesus is a person of compassion who reaches out to people who are forgotten, poor, or outcast. He shows that he has come as a Savior for all people. Everyone is invited to follow him.

This is a Gospel of mercy and forgiveness. Jesus shows us that the Father is loving and merciful. God cares when we're lost and calls us to come back. God will always forgive us and welcome us home. We're also called to ask forgiveness from others and to try to make up for any harm we cause to other people.

We have the opportunity through this Gospel to see Jesus' love for all people. Jesus lives the life he teaches about. We see his ministry as an example for our own lives. We learn that we should have grateful hearts for all God has done for us. Through his life, death, and resurrection, Jesus redeems us and calls us to live the life for which we were created.

Jesus shows us that we are to follow his example by opening our hearts to the needs of others. Jesus challenges us to a new way of thinking. We're not to judge others, but to see their hearts. All people are to be our neighbors. Jesus helps us learn to live his way of love. Our encounter with Jesus Christ changes our lives forever.

Shepherds Keep Watch

LUKE 2:8–20

CHRISTMAS • GOD'S LOVE • GENEROSITY • SERVICE

Now there were shepherds in that region living in the fields and keeping the night watch over their flock. The angel of the Lord appeared to them and the glory of the Lord shone around them, and they were struck with great fear. The angel said to them, "Do not be afraid; for behold, I proclaim to you good news of great joy that will be for all the people. For today in the city of David a savior has been born for you who is Messiah and Lord. And this will be a sign for you: you will find an infant wrapped in swaddling clothes and lying in a manger." And suddenly there was a multitude of the heavenly host with the angel, praising God and saying: "Glory to God in the highest and on earth peace to those on whom his favor rests." When the angels went away from them to heaven, the shepherds said to one another, "Let us go, then, to Bethlehem to see this thing that has taken place, which the Lord has made known to us." So they went in haste and found Mary and Joseph, and the infant lying in the manger. When they saw this, they made known the message that had been told them about this child. All who heard it were amazed by what had been told them by the shepherds. And Mary kept all these things, reflecting on them in her heart. Then the shepherds returned, glorifying and praising God for all they had heard and seen, just as it had been told to them.

. . . .

Introduce the Gospel Story

Were you ever really surprised? What happened? Was it a good feeling?

The shepherds were surprised one night while they were watching their sheep outside Bethlehem. Angels came as messengers from God to tell them that a Savior had been born. The shepherds were amazed and filled with hope.

Share a Meditation

Bow your head and listen to this meditation.

Imagine that you are one of the shepherds in Bethlehem. One night you're on a hillside outside the city keeping your sheep safe. It's very dark, and you're getting sleepy. Suddenly there is a bright light in the sky, and an angel from God appears. You and the other shepherds stare in awe.

The angel speaks: "I bring you Good News of great joy for all people: to you is born this day a Savior. You will find a child lying in a manger." What can this mean, you wonder?

All of a sudden, many angels praise God: "Glory to God in the highest!" Then there is darkness again, and everything is quiet. Soon everyone begins to talk at once. What does this mean? Has a Savior really come to Bethlehem? Some of the shepherds decide to go into Bethlehem. You go with them as they look for the child.

You and the shepherds find a stable at the back of an inn. You go inside and see Mary and Joseph. Just as the angel said, a baby is lying in a manger. It's quiet and peaceful in the stable. This is a holy place. You fall to your knees in front of the child. In your heart, you know that baby came from God, and he has come for all people. You return to the hillside and join the other shepherds in praising God.

Take a moment now to give thanks to God for the wonderful gift who is Christ the Lord. Let your heart be filled with love for God because God loves you.

Now it's time to come back to our group. Do any of you want to share your experience of this story with baby Jesus?

Ask Questions

- *What message did the angel have for the shepherds that night?*
- *Where did the shepherds go?*
- *What did they find?*
- *What did the shepherds do when they came back?*
- *What do we celebrate at Christmas?*
- *Did Jesus come for all of us?*

Reflect and Wrap Up the Discussion

This is a wonderful story of how the angel announced the Good News of Jesus' birth to the shepherds. It reminds us that Jesus came for all people. The shepherds were not people of power or prestige. They were working people who took care of the sheep on the hillsides outside Bethlehem, and yet they are the first witnesses of the Christmas miracle.

The Bethlehem event we celebrate at Christmas is remarkable. God became human to fully share in our lives. This is a story of God's unending love for each of us.

Service Activity

GIVE FAMILY STOCKINGS

Adult Preparation

Ask families to provide stockings and stocking stuffers. Suggest children spend some of their own money on these gifts.

Directions for Children

Some children have to be in the hospital even at Christmas, and their families sometimes stay with them. It is a difficult time for families because they cannot be at home to celebrate Christmas. Today we're going to help families with sick children.

You've brought in items to help fill a Christmas stocking for each family with a sick child this Christmas. Let's fill the stockings with a good mix of items for the family members to share.

This project helps us share at Christmas.

Pray Together

God, Father of all,
it gives us great joy to celebrate
the wonderful gift of Christmas
and all you have done for us.
The birth of Jesus in a humble stable
reminds us that Jesus came for all people,
all races, all nations, rich and poor.
May we remember the message of the angels
to the shepherds on that first Christmas
and give glory to you each day. Amen.

Lost and Found

LUKE 15:1–7

GOD'S LOVE • RECONCILIATION • SIN • FORGIVENESS

The tax collectors and sinners were all drawing near to listen to him, but the Pharisees and scribes began to complain, saying, "This man welcomes sinners and eats with them." So to them he addressed this parable. "What man among you having a hundred sheep and losing one of them would not leave the ninety-nine in the desert and go after the lost one until he finds it? And when he does find it, he sets it on his shoulders with great joy and, upon his arrival home, he calls together his friends and neighbors and says to them, 'Rejoice with me because I have found my lost sheep.' I tell you, in just the same way there will be more joy in heaven over one sinner who repents than over ninety-nine righteous people who have no need of repentance."

Introduce the Gospel Story

Did you ever lose a puzzle piece and look all over for it? Even though you had all the other pieces, didn't you want to find the one that was lost?

This Gospel meditation is about a lesson Jesus taught his followers. Jesus tells us that just as a shepherd looks for a lost sheep, so Jesus looks for us when we turn away from him and get lost. Jesus will always love us and will always look for us. He will rejoice when we are found and come back to him.

Share a Meditation

Concentrate now on listening to this Gospel meditation.

You're in the crowd following Jesus. You're sitting on the grass, listening to what Jesus has to say. You hear the Pharisees complain that Jesus welcomes sinners. You know Jesus cares about all kinds of people.

Jesus begins to tell a story. You listen carefully because his stories help you think about things in a different way. Jesus asks the crowd, "If you had a hundred sheep and lost one of them, wouldn't you leave the other ninety-nine to go after the one that is lost?"

Of course a shepherd would go and look for the lost sheep, you think. But you wonder why Jesus is telling this story. Then you hear Jesus say that God is happy when people come back, just as the shepherd is happy when the lost sheep is found. You know God loves us even when we disobey and sin.

You begin to understand what Jesus was telling the Pharisees. We should care about those who have lost their way. God loves all of us, not just some of us.

We always get another chance with God to get things right. Take a moment now to talk to God. Tell God you're sorry for what you've done wrong. Ask forgiveness for what you haven't done to help other people. Listen to God speak in your heart. God loves you.

Now rejoin our group. Would any of you like to share what God said to you in your heart?

Ask Questions

- In this story, who was lost?
- What did the shepherd do?
- Are shepherds happy when their lost sheep are found?
- How is the shepherd like God?
- Does God always forgive us and welcome us back?
- How can we ask for God's forgiveness?

Reflect and Wrap Up the Discussion

This story is another parable that teaches about God's love. Shepherds took care of sheep out in the field, making sure the sheep had good grass to eat. They stayed out all night keeping the sheep safe from harm.

Jesus shows us that our God is a loving God, just like the shepherd. He looks for us when we're lost and rejoices when we're found. God cares about each of us. He forgives us when we disobey and welcomes us back. We always have another chance with God.

Craft Activity

MAKE FLUFFY SHEEP
Materials
- Copies of sheep pattern
- Markers, crayons, or colored pencils
- Cotton balls
- Glue sticks

Directions for Children
One way to remember this story is with a craft activity.
1. Take one copy of the sheep pattern.
2. Underneath the sheep, write "Jesus loves" and then add your name. This will remind you that Jesus cares about each of us like a shepherd cares about his sheep.
3. Next, glue cotton balls to the sheep to make them fluffy.
4. You can also add details to the scene with markers if you choose.

Take home the sheep and share the story of the lost sheep with your family.

Pray Together

Forgiving Father,
we thank you for your unending love
and care for each one of us.
You look for us when we're lost,
and you rejoice when we're found.
We know you always forgive us
when we come back to you
and ask your forgiveness.
Help us remember that you will
never turn away from us
but will be with us always.
We trust in your mercy and forgiveness
at all times and places. Amen.

Give Thanks to God

LUKE 17:12–19

GOD'S LOVE • HEALING • GRATITUDE • PRAYER

As he was entering a village, ten lepers met (him). They stood at a distance from him and raised their voice, saying, "Jesus, Master! Have pity on us!" And when he saw them, he said, "Go show yourselves to the priests." As they were going they were cleansed. And one of them, realizing he had been healed, returned, glorifying God in a loud voice; and he fell at the feet of Jesus and thanked him. He was a Samaritan. Jesus said in reply, "Ten were cleansed, were they not? Where are the other nine? Has none but this foreigner returned to give thanks to God?" Then he said to him, "Stand up and go; your faith has saved you."

Introduce the Gospel Story

Did you ever do something nice and the person didn't even thank you? Do you always remember to thank people who help you?

Our Gospel story today is about giving thanks to God. Jesus cured ten people who had the terrible disease called leprosy. But only one person came back to say thank you to Jesus. We should be like that person. We have much to be thankful for.

Share a Meditation

Put yourself in the Gospel story.

You are in the crowd following Jesus. As Jesus comes to a village, you hear voices call, "Jesus, have mercy on us!" It's group of ten people with leprosy. You know they're not supposed to come near other people. They have to live away from their family and friends for the rest of their lives.

Jesus has heard them. He tells the people with leprosy to show themselves to the priest. They leave, but on the way you see them stop. They look down at their hands and arms and see that they've been cured. They can go home to their families! They run off toward home. You can't believe it. Jesus cured them!

Then you see that one of them is coming back. He falls to his knees in front of Jesus and thanks him for this wonderful miracle. Jesus says to the crowd, "Were not ten made clean? Where are the other nine?"

Then Jesus looks over at you. Suddenly you realize how many times you haven't given thanks to God for your many blessings. Take just a little time right now to give thanks to God in your heart for the good things in your life.

Open your eyes. Do any of you want to share what you gave thanks for?

Ask Questions

- *Who called out to Jesus?*
- *How many people were there?*
- *What did Jesus do for them?*
- *How many came back?*
- *What did Jesus say?*
- *How can we be like the person who said thank you?*
- *What can we thank God for?*

Reflect and Wrap Up the Discussion

This Gospel reminds us that we should thank God for all God has done for us. God is the creator of our world and everything it. God made all the wonders of the universe for us because God loves us endlessly.

We should have grateful hearts for everything God has done for us. Giving thanks to God is part of who we are as God's people. When things seem difficult for us, we can look around us and see the many gifts God has given us out of love.

Craft Activity

MAKE A BLESSING TREE

Materials

- Brown butcher paper
- Green construction paper
- Markers, crayons, or colored pencils
- Tape
- Scissors

Adult Preparation

1. Use brown butcher paper to create the shape of a large tree with several branches.
2. Hang it on the wall.
3. Write "Our Blessing Tree" on a sheet of paper and hang it on the wall next to the tree.
4. Make copies of the leaf pattern on green paper.

Directions for Children

We can work together to create a blessing tree. God give us many blessings. Let's name some of the things we can thank God for: sunshine, stars, people, trees, flowers, music, food, animals, and God's love. What are some other ideas?

We will make green leaves for the paper tree on the wall. The sign next to it says "Our Blessing Tree."

1. Cut out a leaf for our tree from green paper.
2. On your leaf, print something you're thankful to God for.
3. Put your leaf on the blessing tree by putting tape on the back and sticking it to the tree.

In this way, we remember to give thanks to God.

Pray Together

God of all blessings,
we praise you for all of the gifts you have given us
and the love you have for each of us.
We give thanks for the amazing beauty of all creation.
Most of all we thank you for the gift of one another
and the blessings others bring to our lives.
Help us wisely use the gifts you have given us
for the good of all people. Amen.

Pray From the Heart

LUKE 18:9–14

PRAYER • GOD'S LOVE • FOLLOWING JESUS

He then addressed this parable to those who were convinced of their own righteousness and despised everyone else. "Two people went up to the temple area to pray; one was a Pharisee and the other was a tax collector. The Pharisee took up his position and spoke this prayer to himself, 'O God, I thank you that I am not like the rest of humanity—greedy, dishonest, adulterous—or even like this tax collector. I fast twice a week, and I pay tithes on my whole income.' But the tax collector stood off at a distance and would not even raise his eyes to heaven but beat his breast and prayed, 'O God, be merciful to me a sinner.' I tell you, the latter went home justified, not the former; for everyone who exalts himself will be humbled, and the one who humbles himself will be exalted."

Introduce the Gospel Story

Do you think everything you do is right? Do you think you do good things all by yourself?

This story is about someone who thought he did everything right. It shows us we must realize that everything we do depends on God. Without God we have nothing, because God created everything. But with God, we know all things are possible.

Share a Meditation

Imagine you are with Jesus as he teaches.

You're there listening to him. Jesus is telling a story about a Pharisee and a tax collector who go to the temple to pray. You think Jesus will say we should pray like the Pharisees, who keep every law and are well respected. People hated tax collectors because in those days they cheated people by charging them more than they owed and keeping the extra money for themselves.

The Pharisee prays, "Thank you God that I am not like other people." The tax collector prays, "God, be merciful to me." What Jesus says is a surprise. He says we shouldn't pray like the Pharisee, who focuses on himself. We should be like the tax collector, who prays from his heart. The tax collector asks God's forgiveness. He knows he needs God's help.

You know Jesus wants us to pray from our hearts. How can you ask God for help? Take a moment now to talk to God in your own words, in the silence of your heart.

Now come back to this time and place. Do any of you want to share how you think you can ask God for help?

Ask Questions

- What were the Pharisee and the tax collector doing?
- What did the Pharisee say to God?
- What did the tax collector say to God?
- What did Jesus say about their prayers?
- When we pray, what should we tell God?
- What are some of the ways we can pray?

Reflect and Wrap Up the Discussion

Prayer is part of our relationship with God. You can't be in a relationship with someone you never talk to! Prayer is an important part of being God's people. Our faith in God must be expressed in prayer. We should pray in all we do.

Prayer opens our minds and our hearts to God's presence. Through prayer, we connect with God, who created us and loves us always. When we pray, we must pray from our hearts. We can tell God we're sorry for what we've done wrong and ask for God's help in all things.

Prayer Activity

LEARN PRAYER NAMES FOR GOD
Directions for Children
We can address God with different names in prayer. This expands our understanding of who God is and gives us a variety of ways to pray.

Here are some ways we can begin our prayers: God of glory, Awesome God, Father of all people, God of justice, Lord Jesus, Loving Father, Holy Spirit of love, God of mercy, Lord of light, Spirit of hope, and God of all creation.

Learning different names for God helps us catch a glimpse of who God is. We don't know all God is. Our God is a mighty God who is always with us.

This week, let's use one of our new prayer names for God.

Pray Together

Almighty God,
help us remember that everything we have
and everything we are comes from you.
Help us to be people of prayer in all things
and to remember how much you love us.
Create in us hearts filled with hope
and lives full of love for others. Amen.

Life-Changing Day

LUKE 19:2–10

FOLLOWING JESUS • GOD'S LOVE • SIN • FORGIVENESS

Now a man there named Zacchaeus, who was a chief tax collector and also a wealthy man, was seeking to see who Jesus was; but he could not see him because of the crowd, for he was short in stature. So he ran ahead and climbed a sycamore tree in order to see Jesus, who was about to pass that way. When he reached the place, Jesus looked up and said to him, "Zacchaeus, come down quickly, for today I must stay at your house." And he came down quickly and received him with joy. When they all saw this, they began to grumble, saying, "He has gone to stay at the house of a sinner." But Zacchaeus stood there and said to the Lord, "Behold, half of my possessions, Lord, I shall give to the poor, and if I have extorted anything from anyone I shall repay it four times over." And Jesus said to him, "Today salvation has come to this house because this man too is a descendant of Abraham. For the Son of Man has come to seek and to save what was lost."

Introduce the Gospel Story

Did you ever do something wrong? How did you make up for it?

This Gospel story reminds us that our lives should change when we meet Jesus. We're called to turn our lives around and make up for harm we have caused to others. We must become the kind of people God created us to be.

Share a Meditation

Close your eyes and concentrate on the story. Imagine you are there.

You're in the crowd following Jesus to the town of Jericho. Many people are waiting to see Jesus. Up ahead you see a man climbing a tree so he can see Jesus over the crowd. You recognize this person. His name is Zacchaeus, and he is the chief tax collector. You know he has cheated some of your family and friends.

Jesus has stopped near the tree where Zacchaeus is. You wonder what he's doing. You hear Jesus tell Zacchaeus to come down. Jesus says he will go to his house today. You see Zacchaeus quickly climb down from the tree. They walk to where Zacchaeus lives, and you follow along with some of the others to see what will happen.

Zacchaeus welcomes Jesus inside and gives him something to drink. Zacchaeus tells Jesus he is going to give half his money to the poor and that he's going to repay the money he took by cheating people. In fact, he will pay back four times the money he took.

Wow! You can hardly believe it. Zacchaeus is really changing his life because of Jesus. You think about your life. You realize that Jesus wants us to make up for any trouble we've caused others by our words or actions. How can you do that? Tell Jesus what is in your heart today. Listen to what Jesus says to you.

Then open your eyes. Can any of you share what you said to Jesus?

Ask Questions

- *Who was Zacchaeus?*
- *What did he do to see over the crowd?*
- *Was Zacchaeus an honest person?*
- *What did he promise Jesus he would do?*
- *How are we called to be like Zacchaeus?*
- *Is it easy to ask forgiveness?*
- *Why is it not always enough to say we're sorry?*
- *How can we make up for the wrong we have done?*
- *How can we let Jesus change our lives?*

Reflect and Wrap Up the Discussion

In the story of Zacchaeus, we see how an encounter with Jesus changes one life. We too should be changed by our experience of Jesus. Zacchaeus changes his heart, and our hearts will be transformed if we follow what Jesus teaches.

An interesting part of this story is that Zacchaeus says he will pay back more than he has taken and that he will give to the poor. That shows us that Zacchaeus had been listening to what Jesus taught the people. He knows it's not enough to be sorry. We must also make up for the harm we caused to others.

Craft Activity

CREATE A HAND WREATH

Materials

- Construction paper
- Pencils
- Scissors
- Glue sticks

Adult Preparation

Cut a circle of construction or butcher paper large enough to hold all of the children's paper-hand cutouts.

Directions for Children

We can make a hand wreath together to remind us to live as peacemakers. Jesus wants us to use our hands to help one another, not hurt one another. We are to live as a community of God's people.

1. Choose a piece of construction paper in a bright color.
2. Spread your fingers wide, and then trace around your hand with a pencil to get the outline.
3. Carefully cut out the hand shape.
4. Overlap your paper hand with the one before it, and then glue your hand to that spot on the circle wreath. This will form a hand wreath.

We will display the finished wreath as a reminder that Jesus wants us to reach out our hands to one another in peace and friendship.

Pray Together

Lord Jesus Christ,
we ask your forgiveness for the times we've disobeyed
and for the times we did not help others.
Help us forgive other people and not hold grudges.
Give us loving hearts, that we may live in peace with others.
Hear our prayer and send the Holy Spirit
to guide our hearts and our lives this day. Amen.

From *Plant the Seed: Sharing the Gospel With Children* (Liguori Publications, © 2011 Patricia Mathson). Permission to reproduce granted to original purchaser for noncommercial use only.

Hosanna in the Highest

LUKE 19:28, 36–38

FOLLOWING JESUS • PRAISING GOD
PRAYER • PALM SUNDAY • HOLY WEEK

After he had said this, he proceeded on his journey up to Jerusalem. As he rode along, the people were spreading their cloaks on the road and now as he was approaching the slope of the Mount of Olives, the whole multitude of his disciples began to praise God aloud with joy for all the mighty deeds they had seen. They proclaimed: "Blessed is the king who comes in the name of the Lord. Peace in heaven and glory in the highest."

. . . .

Introduce the Gospel Story

Did you ever go to a parade? Did you have a great time cheering as people went by?

Our Gospel story today is about when Jesus rode into Jerusalem on a donkey. The people honored Jesus by waving palm branches as he went by. They knew he was a great teacher who had helped many people. It's important for us, too, to give praise to Jesus for all he has done for us.

Share a Meditation

Close your eyes and imagine you're there as Jesus enters the city of Jerusalem.

What a great day it is! Many people are getting ready to celebrate Passover. The news is spreading fast about Jesus as a great and wise teacher. People have also heard about the miracles Jesus did for others. They want to see and honor Jesus.

You are with the crowd waiting to greet Jesus as he comes into Jerusalem. You can't believe how many people are here. You can hardly wait for Jesus. You've heard the stories about Jesus, and you think in your heart that he might be the Messiah. You look down the road again. When will Jesus get here?

Finally you see Jesus coming. He is riding on a donkey. When Jesus comes closer, the people give thanks for all the things Jesus has done for them. They shout, "Blessed is the king who comes in the name of the Lord!"

As Jesus passes you, he turns and looks into your eyes. You know that Jesus sees just you at that moment. Then you watch as Jesus continues his journey into the city. You hear people down the road cheer as he comes near.

Now open your heart to Jesus. Give praise to Jesus for all he has done. He has come as a Savior for the world. What do you want to tell Jesus? What does Jesus say to you?

Now, open your eyes as we come back together. Can any of you share what Jesus said to you?

Ask Questions

- *What did the people do when they saw Jesus?*
- *What did they shout to Jesus?*
- *How can we praise Jesus?*
- *Is it important to thank Jesus in prayer?*
- *How can we give praise to Jesus by our actions toward others?*

Reflect and Wrap Up the Discussion

Each year we walk with Jesus to his death and resurrection during Holy Week. The week begins with Palm Sunday and ends with the celebration of Easter. This is the most sacred time of the Church year. We remember all God has done for us through his Son, our Lord Jesus Christ.

As Jesus came into Jerusalem, the people hailed Jesus as a king. They called out, "Blessed is he who comes in the name of the Lord!" Later that week, the people turned against him. This Gospel reminds us to honor Jesus with our words and our actions each day.

Prayer Activity

PRAISE JESUS WITH WORDS AND ACTIONS

Directions for Children

We are called to give praise to Jesus as the people did when Jesus entered Jerusalem. Let's think of some ways to honor the name of Jesus. We can do this with our words and our actions.

We praise Jesus through prayer. We can thank Jesus for all he has done for us. We praise Jesus by lifting our hearts and voices and singing together. We come together to celebrate the Mass on Sunday and learn how to give glory and praise to our Lord Jesus Christ all through the week.

When we follow Jesus' way of love, we give praise to the name of Jesus. When we live as he showed us, we honor his name. When we give a helping hand or forgive someone who has hurt us, we honor Jesus as the Savior of all people.

This week, be sure to praise Jesus at Mass by singing with your full heart and voice. What are some other ways we can praise Jesus this week?

Pray Together

Lord Jesus Christ,
we know the people praised you
on the road to Jerusalem.
They honored you and waved palms
and were excited to see you.
Later that week, they turned against you
despite everything you had done for them.
Help us honor your holy name
in all we say and do each day.
May we never turn away from you,
even when others lose their way.
Give us the strength to be faithful to you.
Hosanna in the highest! Amen.

Alleluia! Alleluia!

LUKE 24:1–12

EASTER • NEW LIFE • GOD'S LOVE • GOOD NEWS

But at daybreak on the first day of the week they took the spices they had prepared and went to the tomb. They found the stone rolled away from the tomb; but when they entered, they did not find the body of the Lord Jesus. While they were puzzling over this, behold, two men in dazzling garments appeared to them. They were terrified and bowed their faces to the ground. They said to them, "Why do you seek the living one among the dead? He is not here, but he has been raised. Remember what he said to you while he was still in Galilee, that the Son of Man must be handed over to sinners and be crucified, and rise on the third day." And they remembered his words. Then they returned from the tomb and announced all these things to the eleven and to all the others. The women were Mary Magdalene, Joanna, and Mary the mother of James; the others who accompanied them also told this to the apostles, but their story seemed like nonsense and they did not believe them. But Peter got up and ran to the tomb, bent down, and saw the burial cloths alone; then he went home amazed at what had happened.

Introduce the Gospel Story

Have you ever received a present you did not expect? Did you wonder what was happening?

That's what happened to the followers of Jesus on the first Easter. In this Gospel story, the women come to the tomb and find that the body of Jesus is not there. Two angels tell them Jesus is alive and has risen! The women get the disciples to come to the tomb too.

Share a Meditation

Listen carefully to this meditation.

It has been a terrible weekend. On Friday, Jesus died on a cross, and it seems like all your hopes and dreams died with him. You get out of bed very early on Sunday morning because you are going with some women to the tomb where Jesus' body had been placed.

It's just getting light when you get near the tomb. Everyone suddenly stops and looks. The large stone that blocked the tomb has been rolled away. Who could have done this? You and the others go inside the tomb and see that Jesus' body isn't there. You wonder what this means.

Two men in a bright light who must be angels say to the women, "Why do you look for the living among the dead? Jesus is not here, but has risen." You hear the words, but you can hardly believe it. Jesus is alive! He has risen from the dead!

You follow the women as they hurry from the tomb. They tell the disciples the Good News. Peter decides to see for himself. He runs to the tomb and looks inside. Peter goes home amazed at what has happened.

You tell everyone you see about what happened at the tomb. You feel happy for the first time in days. Take a moment to talk to the risen Christ. Thank him for all he has done for you. Tell Jesus how you will follow him.

Come back together now. Would any of you like to share what you thanked Jesus for?

Ask Questions

- On what day of the week did this story take place?
- What did the people who went to the tomb see?
- What did the angels say to them?
- What did the women do when they heard Jesus had risen?
- Was Jesus alive?
- How was this possible?
- What does it mean to live as Easter people?

Reflect and Wrap Up the Discussion

We celebrate Easter in the spring, when we see new life all around us. We hear birds sing and see flowers bloom as the Earth is renewed. Easter is a time of hope for all of us. We rejoice because Jesus brings new life to us by his death and resurrection.

The resurrection of Jesus Christ is a sign that everything Jesus said was true. He is the Son of God who came to teach us, redeem us, and bring us new life. We are Easter people. We are to live our faith in the risen Christ each day.

Craft Activity

CREATE EASTER CARDS

Materials
- Construction paper
- Self-stick foam shapes
- Markers, crayons, or colored pencils

Directions for Children

We can share the Good News of Jesus Christ with others by making Easter greeting cards. Think of someone in your life who would enjoy getting a card you made just for him or her.

1. Fold a piece of construction paper in half to make a card.
2. Decorate the front with self-stick foam shapes like flowers and butterflies.
3. Inside the card, print an Easter greeting like "Happy Easter!" or "Alleluia!" and sign your first name.

Help share the joy of Easter by giving the card to someone. In this way, we live as Easter people.

Pray Together

God of new life,
we give you praise and glory for all you have done for us
through your Son, our Lord and Savior Jesus Christ.
Renew our hearts and our lives during this holy Easter season,
that we may live as your followers each day.
May we tell other people the Good News of Jesus Christ,
who brings hope and new life to all of us. Amen.

CHAPTER 4

Sharing the Gospel of John

Share Background With Students

In the Gospel of John, Jesus calls each of us to see who God is through him. Jesus is the Word of God, who was here before the beginning of creation. He is the light of the world we're to follow. Jesus was sent by the Father to teach us, save us, and bring us new life. Jesus shows us God's unending love for us.

We see Jesus at work through the stories of this Gospel. We are to recognize Jesus' presence in our lives and in the lives of others. In what Jesus says and does, we learn the way to the Father. Jesus teaches us how to be his disciples one day at a time. We are to love one another as he has loved us.

We are called to faith in Jesus Christ, who is the Son of God. Faith in Jesus makes us his disciples and calls us to follow where he leads. We are to turn toward the light of Christ. In this way, we live as we were created by our God.

This Gospel calls us to live our lives with faith in the risen Christ in all we do. The words of the Gospel of John call us to life with God, the source of all life. Through the stories of the resurrection, we catch a glimpse of how good God is to us. We must share the Good News with others so that all will come to know our Lord and Savior, Jesus Christ, and believe.

Come and See

JOHN 1:35–46

GOOD NEWS • FOLLOWING JESUS • DISCIPLES • EASTER

The next day John was there again with two of his disciples, and as he watched Jesus walk by, he said, "Behold, the Lamb of God." The two disciples heard what he said and followed Jesus. Jesus turned and saw them following him and said to them, "What are you looking for?" They said to him, "Rabbi" (which translated means Teacher), "where are you staying?" He said to them, "Come, and you will see." So they went and saw where he was staying, and they stayed with him that day. It was about four in the afternoon. Andrew, the brother of Simon Peter, was one of the two who heard John and followed Jesus. He first found his own brother Simon and told him, "We have found the Messiah" (which is translated Anointed). Then he brought him to Jesus. Jesus looked at him and said, "You are Simon the son of John; you will be called Cephas" (which is translated Peter). The next day he decided to go to Galilee, and he found Philip. And Jesus said to him, "Follow me." Now Philip was from Bethsaida, the town of Andrew and Peter. Philip found Nathanael and told him, "We have found the one about whom Moses wrote in the law, and also the prophets, Jesus, son of Joseph, from Nazareth." But Nathanael said to him, "Can anything good come from Nazareth?" Philip said to him, "Come and see."

Introduce the Gospel Story

What Good News do you like to share with other people? Whom do you tell?

In this Gospel story, Jesus invites us to come and see who he is. John the Baptist told others that Jesus was coming. Some of them found Jesus, and he told them, "Come and see." This story speaks to us. Jesus calls each of us to follow him.

Share a Meditation

Close your eyes as you listen to our Gospel meditation. Put yourself in the time of Jesus.

You are with John the Baptist, Andrew, and another disciple. John sees Jesus walk by. He turns and points out that Jesus is the one you seek. A disciple asks Jesus where he is staying. Jesus says, "Come and see."

The disciples go with him, and you hurry to catch up. Later that afternoon, you go with Andrew to find his brother Simon. Andrew tells Simon, "We have found the Messiah!" Andrew brings his brother to Jesus, who smiles and says to Simon, "You will be called Peter." You realize Jesus is giving him a new name for a new life.

The next day, all of you go to Galilee with Jesus. You see him go up to a man named Philip. "Follow me," Jesus says to him. Philip leaves everything behind and goes with Jesus. Later Philip looks for his friend Nathanael. Philip tells him the Good News about Jesus. Philip says to Nathanael, "Come and see."

You begin to see that following Jesus also means sharing the Good News with others. Jesus calls each of us to follow him. We are called to "come and see."

Now, listen for Jesus speaking to you in the silence of your heart. How does Jesus ask you to follow him?

Open your eyes and know that Jesus is with you always. Do any of you want to share how Jesus invited you to follow him?

Ask Questions

- *In this Gospel story, who knew who Jesus was?*
- *What did Jesus say when he saw the disciples following him?*
- *What did Andrew tell his brother?*
- *Why did Jesus give Simon a new name?*
- *What did Philip say to Nathanael?*
- *Who is called to follow Jesus?*
- *How can we tell others about Jesus and his Good News?*

Reflect and Wrap Up the Discussion

It is a daily commitment to live as Jesus' disciple. We're called to faith in the risen Christ who is present among us. He will show us the way to live.

We must also share the Good News with others. We must lead other people to Jesus Christ. We are called to invite everyone to come and see all God has done for us. Look for opportunities to do this today and every day.

Craft Activity

CREATE SHAPE CROSSES

Materials

- Purple craft foam
- Self-stick foam shapes
- Scissors

Adult preparation

Draw a cross pattern on the purple craft foam.

Directions for Children

We can make colorful crosses to take home. They will help us remember to follow Jesus Christ each day.

1. Cut out the cross shape from the purple craft foam.
2. Use self-stick foam shapes such as triangles, circles, squares, and hearts to decorate your cross. Peel the backing off each shape and stick it your cross.

Take home your cross and place it where you will see it. The cross is a symbol of our Lord Jesus Christ. The cross helps us remember that Jesus calls each of us to follow him. We are to walk his way of love each day.

Pray Together

Lord, Jesus,
help us hear your call
and come and see who you are
for us and for all people.
Give us the strength to follow you
even when the way is difficult.
Help us invite others to come and see
the Good News of your love for all people.
May we live always as your disciples
in all we say and do each day,
for with you, all things are possible. Amen.

Sick Child Gets Well

JOHN 4:46–53

HEALING • FAITH • GOD'S LOVE • KINGDOM OF GOD • SERVICE

Now there was a royal official whose son was ill in Capernaum. When he heard that Jesus had arrived in Galilee from Judea, he went to him and asked him to come down and heal his son, who was near death. Jesus said to him, "Unless you people see signs and wonders, you will not believe." The royal official said to him, "Sir, come down before my child dies." Jesus said to him, "You may go; your son will live." The man believed what Jesus said to him and left. While he was on his way back, his slaves met him and told him that his boy would live. He asked them when he began to recover. They told him, "The fever left him yesterday, about one in the afternoon." The father realized that just at that time Jesus had said to him, "Your son will live," and he and his whole household came to believe.

....

Introduce the Gospel Story

Have you ever had to ask for help? Did you know in your heart that the person would help you?

This Gospel story is about a man who believed in Jesus. His son was very ill, but the man had faith that Jesus would cure him. Jesus worked miracles when he was on Earth. These miracles showed the people that he came from God. The miracles gave people a glimpse of the kingdom of God.

Share a Meditation

Bow your head and imagine that you are there with Jesus.

You're walking with Jesus to the town of Cana. It's about one o'clock in the afternoon on a sunny day. You're happy to be with Jesus.

A royal official comes up to Jesus. He tells Jesus his son is very sick and asks Jesus to come and heal his son. You hear Jesus say, "Go, your son will live." The official believes what Jesus says and starts for home.

The next day you see a friend of yours. You tell him about the official who came to ask Jesus to cure his son. Your friend knows the rest of the story. He overheard the official talking to his servants, who had come to tell him his son was getting better.

The official asked them when the boy started getting well. The servants said it was about one o'clock the previous day. The man knew that was when Jesus had said to him, "Your son will live." He believed in Jesus, and so did his whole household.

We, too, are called to have that man's faith in Jesus. We must know in our hearts that Jesus cares about us. Talk now to Jesus. Tell him you believe in him.

Open your eyes as we come back together. Do any of you want to share what you told Jesus?

Ask Questions

- *Who came up to Jesus?*
- *What did the official want from Jesus?*
- *What did Jesus say to him?*
- *Did the man believe Jesus?*
- *Whom did the man see on his way home?*
- *What did the servants tell him?*
- *When did the boy start to get better?*
- *Did others believe because of the official's belief?*
- *Why did Jesus work miracles?*

Reflect and Wrap Up the Discussion

This Gospel story is one of many about Jesus healing people. Jesus was a person of great compassion who reached out to the sick, the outcasts, and the poor. We're to follow Jesus' example in having compassion for others. We're also called to have faith like the official in the story—faith that Jesus will take care of us.

We are witnesses to what Jesus said and did through the words of the Gospels. We are to believe in our Lord Jesus Christ and to know he is the Son of God.

Service Activity

HELP SICK CHILDREN GO TO CAMP

Materials

- Paper or poster board
- Markers
- Collection boxes

Adult Preparation

1. Ask an organization that provides camps or summer activities for children with serious illnesses or disabilities what items they need for their programs. Develop a list to hand out to children.
2. Secure locations to set out collection boxes.
3. Write a headline and details describing the collection on poster board and sheets of paper the children will decorate.
4. Decide whether to have the children work individually decorating the sheets or in groups decorating the posters (or both).
5. Make extra copies of the list for the children to take home.

Directions for Children

It's important to be people of compassion as Jesus was. One way to show our compassion is to help sick children.

There are camps where children with serious illnesses can go and have fun. We can collect items for these camps. Today we're going to decorate signs to help organize our collection.

[Give instructions based on step 4 above.]

We'll hang these signs by the collection boxes.

Today when you get home, ask your families and friends to donate items for the collection. They should donate things on the list of needed supplies.

This is one way to reach out to children who deal with serious illness every day. Let's also remember to pray for all children who are dealing with health issues. May they know that God is always with them.

Pray Together

Lord Jesus Christ,
help us have compassion for other people
and follow your example
of love and service for others.
You helped the sick of all ages,
and you call us to lend a helping hand
to others in your holy name.
Fill our hearts with your love,
that we may share that love with others,
especially the sick. Amen.

From *Plant the Seed: Sharing the Gospel With Children* (Liguori Publications, © 2011 Patricia Mathson).
Permission to reproduce granted to original purchaser for noncommercial use only.

Serve Others Like Jesus

JOHN 13:2–17

SERVICE • FOLLOWING JESUS
LOVING OUR NEIGHBOR • HOLY THURSDAY

The devil had already induced Judas, son of Simon the Iscariot, to hand him over. So, during supper, fully aware that the Father had put everything into his power and that he had come from God and was returning to God, he rose from supper and took off his outer garments. He took a towel and tied it around his waist. Then he poured water into a basin and began to wash the disciples' feet and dry them with the towel around his waist. He came to Simon Peter, who said to him, "Master, are you going to wash my feet?" Jesus answered and said to him, "What I am doing, you do not understand now, but you will understand later." Peter said to him, "You will never wash my feet." Jesus answered him, "Unless I wash you, you will have no inheritance with me." Simon Peter said to him, "Master, then not only my feet, but my hands and head as well." Jesus said to him, "Whoever has bathed has no need except to have his feet washed, for he is clean all over; so you are clean, but not all." For he knew who would betray him; for this reason, he said, "Not all of you are clean." So when he had washed their feet (and) put his garments back on and reclined at table again, he said to them, "Do you realize what I have done for you? You call me 'teacher' and 'master,' and rightly so, for indeed I am. If I, therefore, the master and teacher, have washed your feet, you ought to wash one another's feet. I have given you a model to follow, so that as I have done for you, you should also do. Amen, amen, I say to you, no slave is greater than his master nor any messenger greater than the one who sent him. If you understand this, blessed are you if you do it."

Introduce the Gospel Story

Did someone ever do something unexpected for you? Did it turn out to be a good thing?

In this Gospel story, Jesus does something unexpected for his disciples. He washes their feet! Jesus does this to teach the disciples to be servants of others. He is an example for all generations of how we are to live.

Share a Meditation

As we begin our meditation, close your eyes. Listen to the story.

You are with Jesus and his disciples in Jerusalem. You had a meal together, and now everyone is talking. You see Jesus get up from the table. He ties a towel around his waist. He gets a jug of water and pours the water into a big bowl. You have no idea why he is doing this.

Jesus goes over to one of his disciples. He sets the bowl of water on the floor and begins to wash the man's feet and dry them with the towel. Feet get so dirty because the roads are dusty and everyone wears sandals. You think Jesus shouldn't have to do that. You look over at Peter. He is watching Jesus. He can't believe it either.

After Jesus washes the disciples' feet, he sits with them around the table again. He tells his disciples, "So if I, your Lord, have washed your feet, you ought to wash one another's feet." Jesus continues, "For I have given you an example. You should do as I have done."

You begin to understand that Jesus did not come to be a king. Rather he shows us that true leaders share God's love by serving others. The thing is, you're not sure how you're going to be able to wash everyone else's feet.

Then you realize the message isn't that we have to wash each others' feet. It's that we are to serve others as Jesus did. This is the challenge of the Good News.

What does this message mean for you? Tell Jesus what you'll do to serve others. Then listen for Jesus to speak to you in the silence of your heart.

Open your eyes now. Do any of you want to share how you'll serve others?

Ask Questions

> In this Gospel story, where were Jesus and his disciples?

> What did Jesus do after dinner?

> Why did he wash his disciples' feet?

> What does Jesus want us to do?

> What are some ways to serve others like Jesus?

Reflect and Wrap Up the Discussion

In this Gospel story, Jesus teaches his disciples by words *and* example. He washes their feet. He shows us that we must serve others because he was the servant of all, and following Jesus means living as he lived.

Jesus teaches us to care about other people. Faith in Jesus means opening our hearts to the needs of others. Only in this way do we become the kind of people God created us to be from the beginning.

Service Activity

MAKE GIFT CERTIFICATES

Materials
- Drawing paper
- Markers, crayons, or colored pencils

Directions for Children

Let's think of ways to serve others.

We're going to make service gift certificates to give to people. There are many ways to help others, including set the table for dinner, clean up the play area at home, help another child study, or play a younger child's favorite game

1. Put the words "Gift Certificate" at the top of a sheet of paper. Under that, write the name of the person who will get the certificate.
2. Next, write the favor you will do for that person.
3. Decorate the certificate to make it beautiful and special.
4. Sign your name at the bottom.

This is a way to show care for others by our actions. We can serve others as Jesus teaches us. In this way, we live his message of love.

Pray Together

Lord Jesus Christ,
when you washed your disciples' feet,
you showed us what it means to love other people.
Open our hearts and our lives to the needs of others.
Give us the courage to walk always in faith, hope, and love.
May we serve others as you were the servant of all. Amen.

Love One Another

JOHN 13:33–35

GOD'S LOVE • LOVING OUR NEIGHBOR
SERVICE • HOLY THURSDAY

My children, I will be with you only a little while longer. You will look for me, and as I told the Jews, "Where I go you cannot come," so now I say it to you. I give you a new commandment: love one another. As I have loved you, so you also should love one another. This is how all will know that you are my disciples, if you have love for one another.

....

Introduce the Gospel Story

Do you care about others? How do you help other people?

We are called to live the Gospels. To do this, we must reflect on what Jesus tells us. This Gospel story is about Jesus' command to love one another. We are to care about others as Jesus cares about us.

Share a Meditation

Bow your head and put yourself in the Gospel story with Jesus.

It has been a remarkable day for Jesus' disciples. He shared a special meal with them, and then he washed their feet! Who could ever have imagined this?

You hear Jesus tell the disciples he will not be with them much longer. You wonder why. You listen carefully to what else Jesus has to say to those in the room that night. Jesus says, "Just as I have loved you, you also should love one another."

You know that love is at the heart of Jesus' message. He tells us how much God loves us and that we are to share that love with others. Jesus shows God's love for each person by his words and his actions. You have seen his compassion for people who are sick or poor.

You think it will be very difficult to love others as much as Jesus does. But he isn't finished yet. He says, "By this everyone will know that you are my disciples, if you have love for one another." You realize other people will judge what Jesus had to say by what we do and say as followers of Jesus.

As you think about all this, Jesus comes toward you. He sits down beside you. Talk to Jesus. Tell him what is in your heart. Listen for what Jesus says to you.

Come back to this time and place. Do any of you want to share what Jesus told you?

Ask Questions

- *How much did Jesus say we are to love others?*
- *Can we choose whom we are to love?*
- *Why is it difficult to love some people?*
- *Does Jesus call us to love them anyway?*
- *How do people see Jesus through us?*
- *What are ways we can show love with our words and actions?*

Reflect and Wrap Up the Discussion

Jesus knew this would be the last time he would see his disciples before he was put to death on a cross. He tells his disciples that we are to love one another. It sounds so simple to say, yet Jesus' words and actions show it's not always easy to love others. People can be against us even when we're doing the right thing.

It's a challenge to live the way of love Jesus showed us. Jesus calls us to share God's love with other people. This love is given to us to be shared with others. We were created to live in a community and to love one another. We can pray and ask for Jesus' help when it's hard to do this.

Craft Activity

CREATE MOSAIC HEARTS

Materials

- Sheets of red craft foam
- Sheets of self-stick foam in other colors
- Scissors
- Printer-ready self-stick labels

Adult Preparation

1. Cut out large hearts from the red craft foam.
2. Cut the self-stick foam into small squares.
3. Use a word-processing program to create and print labels that say "Love one another."

Directions for Children

Hearts are a symbol of love. We can make mosaic hearts to take home as a reminder to live in love as Jesus teaches by his word and example.

1. Stick the label on your red foam heart.
2. Decorate the heart using the colorful squares of self-stick foam. You can have more of one color and less of another. Place the colorful squares onto the heart in any arrangement to make a terrific mosaic heart.

Take your mosaic heart home as a reminder that God called us to love one another as God loves us.

Pray Together

Lord, Jesus Christ,
you call us to follow in your footsteps
and love one another as you love us.
Give us the strength to look beyond
our own need to the needs of others.
Guide our hearts and our lives,
that we may live in love today and always. Amen.

From *Plant the Seed: Sharing the Gospel With Children* (Liguori Publications, © 2011 Patricia Mathson). Permission to reproduce granted to original purchaser for noncommercial use only.

What a Wonderful Day

JOHN 20:11–18

EASTER • PRAISING GOD • NEW LIFE • SERVICE

But Mary stayed outside the tomb weeping. And as she wept, she bent over into the tomb and saw two angels in white sitting there, one at the head and one at the feet where the body of Jesus had been. And they said to her, "Woman, why are you weeping?" She said to them, "They have taken my Lord, and I don't know where they laid him." When she had said this, she turned around and saw Jesus there, but did not know it was Jesus. Jesus said to her, "Woman, why are you weeping? Whom are you looking for?" She thought it was the gardener and said to him, "Sir, if you carried him away, tell me where you laid him, and I will take him." Jesus said to her, "Mary!" She turned and said to him in Hebrew, "Rabbouni," which means Teacher. Jesus said to her, "Stop holding on to me, for I have not yet ascended to the Father. But go to my brothers and tell them, 'I am going to my Father and your Father, to my God and your God.'" Mary of Magdala went and announced to the disciples, "I have seen the Lord," and what he told her.

Introduce the Gospel Story

Did you ever have a great day? Why was it such a terrific day?

In this Gospel story, Mary Magdalene comes to the tomb and finds Jesus' body missing. It turns out to be a wonderful day when she sees the risen Christ. We, too, rejoice at Easter, for the presence of the risen Christ is among us. Easter is a glorious celebration of all God has done for us!

Share a Meditation

Close your eyes. Imagine you're in Jerusalem on the first Easter Sunday.

You're quietly standing a short way from the empty tomb where they had laid Jesus' body. Ever since Good Friday, you've thought about the events of that day. You can't get them out of your mind. How could this have happened?

You hear someone crying. It's Mary Magdalene. She found that the big stone was rolled away from the front of the tomb. Jesus' body was gone! You wonder where Jesus has been taken. You feel like crying too.

Then you see Mary Magdalene talking to someone. You think it might be the gardener. "Mary," he says. You see the look of joy on Mary Magdalene's face. You look closer at the man. It's Jesus! He's alive! Your heart is filled with hope. What an amazing day this is!

You hear Jesus tell Mary Magdalene to tell the disciples about what has happened. You hurry after her. She announces to the disciples, "I have seen the Lord!" Five wonderful words. Jesus has risen as he said he would.

We too must look for the risen Christ's presence. We are called to share the Good News as Mary Magdalene did. Jesus is risen, and we know that all he taught is true.

Talk now to Jesus in your heart. Tell him how you will share the Good News with others.

Now open your eyes. Can anyone share how you told Jesus you would share the Good News?

Ask Questions

- *In this Gospel story, where was Mary Magdalene?*
- *Why was she crying?*
- *Whom did she see in the garden?*
- *Did she know it was Jesus?*
- *What did she ask him?*
- *What did Jesus tell her to do?*
- *What did she say to the disciples?*

Reflect and Wrap Up the Discussion

The story of Mary Magdalene in the garden is our story too. Jesus' resurrection is at the heart of our faith in God. We are Easter people called to live in hope. We're to recognize the risen Christ's presence in our lives. Sometimes we find him in unexpected places and in unexpected people, but we must always be looking for Jesus.

We are called to share the Good News of the risen Christ with others. We must show people that our world can become a better place if we believe in Jesus and follow his way.

Service Activity

LIVE AS EASTER PEOPLE

Directions for Children

We are to live as Easter people. This means living as Jesus showed us by his words and example.

Let's talk about some ways we can do this. We can say "have a good day" to someone on the way out of Mass, listen when someone needs to talk, invite someone to sit with us at lunch, or make a donation to a charity.

Each of us has something to offer. This week, do something that shows you're living in the light of the risen Jesus.

We are people of the resurrection. By sharing the Good News of Jesus Christ, we can bring hope to others. We can make a difference one person at a time.

Pray Together

God of all people,
thank you for sending Jesus to us
as Teacher and Redeemer.
We rejoice in all you've done
out of love for each of us.
Help us share the Good News of Easter
with other people near and far. Amen.

Thomas Believes Jesus

JOHN 20:24–29

EASTER • FOLLOWING JESUS • FAITH • PRAISING GOD

Thomas, called Didymus, one of the Twelve, was not with them when Jesus came. So the other disciples said to him, "We have seen the Lord." But he said to them, "Unless I see the mark of the nails in his hands and put my finger into the nailmarks and put my hand into his side, I will not believe." Now a week later his disciples were again inside and Thomas was with them. Jesus came, although the doors were locked, and stood in their midst and said, "Peace be with you." Then he said to Thomas, "Put your finger here and see my hands, and bring your hand and put it into my side, and do not be unbelieving, but believe." Thomas answered and said to him, "My Lord and my God!" Jesus said to him, "Have you come to believe because you have seen me? Blessed are those who have not seen and have believed."

Introduce the Gospel Story

Were you ever afraid that something you wanted wouldn't come true? Were you happy when it did?

Thomas was like that. He had followed Jesus. Now that Jesus had died on a cross, he didn't know what to think. In this Gospel story, we hear how Thomas saw Jesus and believed. We, too, are called to believe in Jesus Christ, who has brought all of us new life.

Share a Meditation

Forget for a few minutes about whatever is on your mind. Sit quietly and listen to this Gospel story.

Imagine you're in the upper room with the disciples. Thomas comes in, and you are with him. Neither of you were there when the disciples saw Jesus.

A disciple comes up and says, "We have seen the Lord!" But Thomas isn't sure about that, and neither are you. It seems so hard to believe.

Thomas says, "Unless I see the mark of the nails in his hands, I will not believe." Nothing anyone says can change his mind. You want to believe Jesus is risen. But like Thomas, you have doubts.

A week later, everyone has come together again. The disciples are talking about Jesus, when all of a sudden he's there. Jesus says, "Peace be with you." You look in amazement at the risen Christ. Can this really be true? You see Jesus go over to Thomas.

Jesus says to him, "Do not doubt, but believe." Thomas says to Jesus, "My Lord and my God." You know without a doubt that Jesus is risen. Your heart fills with joy. Jesus is truly the Messiah!

Talk now to the risen Christ in your heart and tell him you believe in him. Open your heart to him and to what he has to say to you.

Now open your eyes and come back together. Would any of you like to share what Jesus said to you?

Ask Questions

> Which disciple was not with the others when they saw Jesus?
> What did the disciples tell Thomas?
> Why didn't Thomas believe them?
> When did Thomas believe that Jesus had risen?
> What did Thomas say to Jesus?
> Why are these words our prayer too?

Reflect and Wrap Up the Discussion

Thomas doubted that Jesus had really risen until he saw it for himself just as the other disciples had. Then Thomas said, "My Lord and my God." With these words he proclaims his faith in Jesus Christ.

These words are to be our prayer, too. We are called to make an act of faith in Jesus Christ and to witness to all he said and did, even if it is hard for us to believe.

We know Jesus is here with us. We must be open to the presence of the risen Christ and go out and share the Gospel with others.

Craft Activity

MAKE A COLORFUL BUTTERFLY

Materials
- Sheets of craft foam
- Self-stick craft-foam shapes
- Scissors

Adult Preparation

Cut butterfly shapes from the sheets of craft foam.

Directions for Children

Jesus brought new life to each of us by his life, death, and resurrection. The butterfly is a symbol of new life because it appears in the spring when the world is made new. Let's make colorful butterflies as a reminder of the Easter season and all it means.

1. Take one foam butterfly and some self-stick shapes.
2. Design your own butterfly with the shapes and colors you like.

Each butterfly will be a colorful reminder of the new life of Easter. Display your butterfly at home as a sign of the new life of the Easter season.

Pray Together

Awesome God and Father,
we give you praise and thanks
for all you have done for us
through the life, death, and resurrection
of our Lord Jesus Christ.
Hear our prayers that we may have faith in you,
hope in the future, and love for all people.
Renew our hearts and our lives this Easter season
that we may give glory and honor to your name
by the way we live each day. Alleluia!

From *Plant the Seed: Sharing the Gospel With Children* (Liguori Publications, © 2011 Patricia Mathson). Permission to reproduce granted to original purchaser for noncommercial use only.

Big Catch of Fish

JOHN 21:2–12

EASTER • FAITH • FOLLOWING JESUS

Together were Simon Peter, Thomas called Didymus, Nathanael from Cana in Galilee, Zebedee's sons, and two others of his disciples. Simon Peter said to them, "I am going fishing." They said to him, "We also will come with you." So they went out and got into the boat, but that night they caught nothing. When it was already dawn, Jesus was standing on the shore; but the disciples did not realize that it was Jesus. Jesus said to them, "Children, have you caught anything to eat?" They answered him, "No." So he said to them, "Cast the net over the right side of the boat and you will find something." So they cast it, and were not able to pull it in because of the number of fish. So the disciple whom Jesus loved said to Peter, "It is the Lord." When Simon Peter heard that it was the Lord, he tucked in his garment, for he was lightly clad, and jumped into the sea.   The other disciples came in the boat, for they were not far from shore, only about a hundred yards, dragging the net with the fish. When they climbed out on shore, they saw a charcoal fire with fish on it and bread. Jesus said to them, "Bring some of the fish you just caught." So Simon Peter went over and dragged the net ashore full of one hundred fifty-three large fish. Even though there were so many, the net was not torn. Jesus said to them, "Come, have breakfast." And none of the disciples dared to ask him, "Who are you?" because they realized it was the Lord.

Introduce the Gospel Story

Have you ever had something wonderful happen to you? What was it?

This Gospel story is about something wonderful that happened to the disciples. A difficult night turned into a great day. The disciples saw Jesus Christ and knew he was with them. How happy they were that day to recognize Jesus on the shore of the lake! We, too, must look for the risen Christ, who is already with us.

Share a Meditation

Close your eyes and see yourself in this story.

Imagine you are with some of the disciples. Peter is there and tells the others he is going fishing. You and the others decide to go with him. You stay out all night on the boat, but no one catches any fish.

At dawn you decide to head for shore. It has been a long night. As the boat heads in, you see a man on the shore. None of you recognize him. The man tells them, "Cast the net to the right side of the boat, and you will find some fish."

You think this won't work—you've been trying all night. But the disciples decide to try just one more time. You help throw the big fishing net into the water. Suddenly the net is so full of fish you can't pull it back in the boat! Just then the disciple Jesus loved says to Peter, "It is the Lord!" Peter jumps into the water and starts swimming to shore. You and the other disciples come behind Peter in the boat, dragging the net full of fish.

When you get off the boat, you see that the man you hadn't recognized is Jesus! He has a fire going and tells your group to bring some of the fish you've caught. Jesus says to all of you, "Come and have breakfast." He gives each of you some bread and fish. You're all happy because you know the man is Jesus.

You sit next to Jesus at the fire. What do you say to him? Do you tell him you believe in him? Do you thank him for all he has done for you? Do you ask him to help you live in faith each day? Talk to Jesus and tell him what is in your heart. Hear him speak to you.

Now open your eyes.

Ask Questions

> * In this Gospel story, why were the disciples on the lake?
> * Did they catch any fish on their own?
> * What did the man on shore tell them to do?
> * What happened when they cast their net for the last time?
> * What did Peter do when they recognized Jesus?
> * Why were the disciples happy?
> * How do we see Jesus at work in our lives?

Reflect and Wrap Up the Discussion

In this Gospel story, the disciples have been fishing all night and haven't caught any fish. They follow Jesus' call to try again, and this time they catch many, many fish. Later these same fishermen will also catch many followers for the Lord. With the Holy Spirit's help, the disciples become a strong group of people who carry the message of Jesus to the world.

We can learn from this story not to become discouraged and give up, because Jesus is always with us. This can be a challenge when things don't go our way. But we are called to have faith in Jesus in all times and all places.

Role-Play Activity

ACT THE STORY
Volunteers Needed
- Jesus
- Disciple Jesus loved (John)
- Peter
- Several other disciples

Directions for Children

It's fun to act this Gospel story as it is read from the Bible. Acting it helps us remember the story. No one needs to learn lines, because there are only actions. Who wants to volunteer to be Jesus, Peter, John, and the other disciples?

Let's talk about some of the actions in this story: getting in a boat, rowing, fishing by throwing out a net, seeing someone on shore, trying it again, trying to pull in the heavy net, recognizing Jesus, and going to him on shore.

While I read the story out loud, you do the actions.

We can also act this story for a group of younger children. In this way, we share the Gospel with them.

Pray Together

Lord Jesus Christ,
may we live as people of hope in you
because of all you've done for us.
Help us see your presence and love
each day and know you are
with us always, as you said you would be.
Guide our hearts
so we may follow you and
live the challenge of the Gospels.
May we remember that with you,
all things are possible. Amen.

A Guide for Parents and Teachers

Celebrating the Gospels
A Guide for Parents and Teachers
Gaynell Cronin

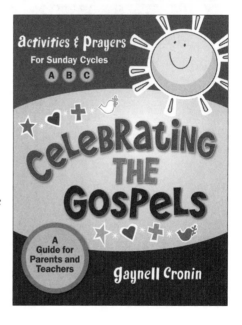

Celebrating the Gospels is written in clear and concise language, with a simple and direct focus for each Gospel. Great for use in family activities, this book allows the whole family, even younger children, to experience the Gospel each week. Parishes can offer studies in which the whole family can attend, and have just one book for each family that can be used for all 3 cycles. Included as well are four special celebrations—Christmas, Epiphany, Easter, and Pentecost.

184-page paperback – 8½" x 11"

978-0-7648-0935-4 • $16.99

My Sister Is Annoying
and Other Prayers for Children
Fr. Joe Kempf with Big Al

My Sister is Annoying! is a beautifully illustrated, fun way for children to talk to God about things that are important to them. Read the prayers and listen to the CD with a child you love as Father Joe and Big Al introduce these prayers read by children.

48-page hardcover with audio CD – 8 x 8
978-0-7648-1827-1 • $16.99

You Want Me to Be Good All Day?
and Other Prayers for Children
Fr. Joe Kempf with Big Al

The follow-up to the best-selling *My Sister Is Annoying!* is introduced by Annie (Big Al's "annoying" sister) and addresses some of the challenges of growing up.

Prayers about Baptism, Communion, and even a wedding make this book perfect for young children beginning to understand what the Church and Sacraments are all about.

48-page hardcover with audio CD – 8 x 8
978-0-7648-1843-1 • $16.99